University of London
Institute of Commonwealth Studies

COMMONWEALTH PAPERS

General Editor
Professor W. H. Morris-Jones

19
Patterns of Administrative Development
in Independent India

COMMONWEALTH PAPERS

Patterns of
Administrative Development
in Independent India

by

E. N. MANGAT RAI

UNIVERSITY OF LONDON

Published for the
Institute of Commonwealth Studies

THE ATHLONE PRESS

1976

Published by
THE ATHLONE PRESS
UNIVERSITY OF LONDON
at 4 *Gower Street, London* WC1

Distributed by Tiptree *Book Services Ltd*
Tiptree, Essex

U.S.A. and Canada
Humanities Press Inc
New Jersey

© *University of London* 1976

ISBN 0 485 17619 X

Printed in Great Britain by
WESTERN PRINTING SERVICES LTD
BRISTOL

CONTENTS

FOREWORD

This latest administrative memoir in the *Commonwealth Papers* series is more comprehensive in scope than those contributed earlier by Sir Charles Jeffries and Professor Michael Dei-Anang. Mr E. N. Mangat Rai entered the Indian Civil Service in 1937 and retired in 1971. During his service he worked at district, state, and central government levels with two notable periods as Chief Secretary to the Governments of Punjab and Kashmir. In the light of his varied experience he illustrates and reflects upon the changes in administrative practice in the largest of the 'new states' from the later imperial period through the first twenty-four years of independent India. It is a study which illumines the problems of governance in India and the processes of change in one of the world's important bureaucracies.

Mr Mangat Rai's attachment to the Institute for the period of work on this book was made possible by a grant from the Nuffield Foundation to whom we wish to express our thanks.

W. H. M-J.

PREFACE

I am indebted to two educational institutions for providing me with the opportunity to write this book. The Institute of Commonwealth Studies, University of London, invited me to do so, and I enjoyed all its facilities from January to August 1974. The Institute was given a grant for this purpose by the Nuffield Foundation.

I had the use of a flat, at a reasonable rent, from William Goodenough House, in central, quiet, and beautiful Mecklenburgh Square. I was within walking distance of London University and most of my other interests. This saved time and expense on travel, and my surroundings were an inducement to concentration, though I must confess also to the constant temptation to walk into the Square garden, particularly on sunny days, of which there were I believe more than average during my visit.

It has been of great value to write this book removed from the pressures of the Indian environment. This has helped in gaining perspective and evaluating my subject more steadily and as a whole. I had the benefit of papers and seminars, as well as informal discussions, with some of the knowledgeable and stimulating persons who work at, or visit, London University. I have been constantly surprised at their insight and familiarity with Indian subjects, and have had need to re-examine assumptions, and knowledge, I had taken for granted.

Two other institutions have unwittingly helped me. I was privileged to live for four months, preceding my arrival in London, in the broad and pleasant acres of the Southern Methodist University at Dallas, Texas, which was a fruitful period of thinking out my subject and writing a rough draft. On arrival in England, in January, I was immediately afflicted with a severe bout of pneumonia, and admitted to University College Hospital. I experienced for the first time the benefits of Britain's National Health Service; I could not have been in better hands, or more considerately restored to health.

Professor W. H. Morris-Jones, Director of the Institute of Commonwealth Studies, initiated the idea that I should attempt a 'distillation', as he called it, of my experience as an administrator. He has stood firmly by me in assistance of all kinds, both personal and connected with the project. He, Dr Hugh Tinker, and Mr J. M. Lee at the Institute, were kind enough to read my first, rather long and rambling, draft, and give me their meticulous and frank advice and criticism. The views expressed are my own; any improvements in presentation are shared with them.

I am grateful to Nayantara Sahgal for working through the whole of the manuscript at every stage of its preparation. She crossed the i's and dotted the t's with rigorous, even ruthless, application, ignoring my many expressions of impatience.

Colleagues of mine in India, particularly Mr A. S. Bhatia, Mr B. B. Vohra, and Mr A. P. Verma, with whom I have had the privilege to work at various times, supplied me by correspondence with some of the detailed factual information I needed.

Mrs Ann Oakley, Mrs Anne Barnes, and Miss Yvonne Crawford typed the various drafts of the manuscript with speed and accuracy.

Last but by no means least I wish to thank 'England's green and pleasant land' for its renewed hospitality, and the many gifts a sojourn here has always given me.

London   E. N. Mangat Rai
June 1974

INTRODUCTION

This book is not autobiography, nor an analysis of the whole sphere of Indian administration. It includes, however, some aspects of both. It attempts to trace developments in administration which have come within my personal experience during my career as an administrator from the last decade of British rule through the independence years. Its scope is in this way limited and practical, not comprehensive and theoretical.

I entered the Indian Civil Service (ICS) through the London competitive examination of 1937. After a year's training at Oxford I worked in the ICS for thirty-three years. I was allotted to the province of the Punjab, which was partitioned at independence between India and Pakistan, when I opted to work in the Indian Punjab (now called state), the frontiers of which have changed more than once, even after the partition of 1947, following the reorganization of states within India. In 1964 I was transferred to Jammu and Kashmir state as its Chief Secretary, and in 1967 to the Union central government as Special Secretary in the Ministry of Petroleum and Chemicals. I resigned from the ICS at the end of 1971 following a disagreement with the Union government arising from a personnel case.

It has been difficult to decide, for a treatment of this kind, whether it was better to deal with individual subjects or themes as illustrative of the administrative process, or to follow broadly a description of the kinds of problems encountered in the various positions I held. I have concluded that there is advantage in the latter method, as it provides a picture of the concrete administrative situation in which particular subjects arose and were dealt with. I have, therefore, in Chapters 2 to 9 followed sequentially my career in the civil service. These chapters generally include in their titles dates which are the years when I was associated in positions of administrative responsibility with the subject matter of the chapter. The only exception to this is Chapter 7, where a personality, Chief Minister Partap Singh Kairon, dominates the administrative scene. I was in fact Chief Secretary to the Punjab government, working in direct responsibility to Kairon from 1957 to 1962.

This manner of presenting the material also has a considerable disadvantage. The wood may well be lost for the trees, and it will try the reader's patience and interest to go through a series of chapters not intrinsically connected with each other nor each dealing with a particular administrative theme. I feel, however, that this presents a more realistic picture of the administration as it actually worked. It will be seen that an important feature of both methods and performance has been variety and unevenness, even eccentricity.

Nonetheless, there are trends which stand out and may be disentangled and defined, marking distinct changes in administrative methods, values, and styles. I attempt to deal with some general aspects in this introduction and with more specific changes in Chapter 10.

I have deliberately kept the autobiographical and the subjective to a minimum. I have not dealt in terms of 'I', nor described my particular reactions to events or people. These were indeed a world in themselves in aspiration, in achievement, often in defeat and heartbreak. Nor is this surprising; my generation of civil servants, after all, was associated with the great task of helping our ancient land to become a modern nation. In Chapters 2 to 9 I have certainly, though briefly, raised issues or described attitudes but generally not pushed these to a conclusion or thesis. I have allowed myself greater liberty in the first and last chapters, and have included three Appendices, beyond the strict scope of this book, where the subject or the trend of events seemed important enough to merit comment, and had significance in terms of my experience as an administrator.

It seems useful to indicate selectively the main trends of change and development in administration in independent India to provide a perspective to the details which follow. This book is not concerned with a description of the many gigantic problems facing India in establishing itself successfully as an independent country, even though these were the background for the administration. India had practised administrative unity under imperial rule; this unity had to be converted to one also supported by the will of its people. This included a settlement with the Indian princely states, to be absorbed and then integrated into the political, constitutional, and administrative system. India decided on a democratic, federal government, involving most intricate and delicate relationships and the balancing of forces of a divisive, regional type, as well as grave disparities in income and well-being between classes and castes and between areas of the country. India was the largest democracy in the world, also the poorest; its middle class was infinitesimal, though of crucial importance as the repository of education and know-how. India's languages, cultures, and castes were more various than those any federal order had attempted anywhere in the world, at any time in history, to weld in freedom into the working cohesion of a single union. At independence it was faced overnight with the movement of millions and a giant problem of relief and rehabilitation, and following this, a confrontation with Pakistan in October 1947.

These were only some of the problems. Each one had a political content, but each also had an administrative complement of large dimensions.

The period since independence has witnessed vast changes in administration. The broad development has been away from the monolithic, strictly hierarchical, administration, with the line of command running unimpeded from the Viceroy in Delhi to the furthest village, to variegated patterns of administrative organization and effort. This is particularly evident in expressions of the federal structure in the states. Each state has a personality of its own; these are no longer merely chunks of territory for administrative purposes. The number, size, and composition of states has been changed several times to conform with the demands of the people in their search for identity. Another manifest expression of diversity is that various branches of the administration, even in the same state or at the Union, are no longer controlled by a single dominating civil service. There is no common or personnel link between judiciary and executive, between technical experts in engineering and other subjects on the one hand and the generalist administrators of the ICS and its successor, the Indian Administrative Service (IAS) on the other.

Thus vast and continuous processes of decentralization, diversification, and even diffusion and disintegration mark the change in administrative methods in India. This book will consider some of these in detail. This movement was inevitable, indeed even welcome and necessary for healthy development, in an administration which based itself firmly on a federal system and democratic responsible governments. But the process has equally inevitably created new problems of coordination and integration, and of discovering ways of directing the administrative effort to common and comprehended goals, or even to different goals in an orderly and sustained manner.

This coordination has been provided during this period by the political will. Institutional and individual manifestations of this will are discussed in some of the chapters that follow. Suffice it here to mention that these have been many and various, from parliamentary and state legislatures to the Five-Year Plans, the influence and at times dominating economic authority of the Planning Commission, the party system, particularly the influence of the Indian National Congress, and even the individual personalities of politicians, specially in the states, such as Morarji Desai, the Chief Minister of Bombay (1952–57), Partap Singh Kairon of the Punjab (1956–64), Kamraj of Madras (now Tamil Nadu) (1953–63), Biju Patnaik of Orissa (1961–63), and Bakshi Ghulam Mohammad of Jammu and Kashmir (1953–64), to mention only a few.

The thesis here is that the political will, however variously operated, has been the crucial factor in administrative developments and performance in independent India. The Indian administration was, in that sense, in politics from zero hour, 15 August 1947.

In the administrative developments that have taken place, primarily in response to expressions of political will, it is difficult, even futile, to fix dates for particular changes. The process has been continuous. It is perhaps possible, however, to recognize three phases in the period since 1947, in each of which the character of the political forces and their impact on the administration has changed.

The period 1947–57 represents administratively a remarkably smooth change from the British Raj to a parliamentary system. The political will was expressed, for lack of a better term, in the best liberal British tradition of government. The outward and visible sign was the Constitution of India, which was finally signed, sealed, and delivered to the Indian people by their representatives in the Constituent Assembly on 26 January 1950. In this period the administrative system was largely insulated from day to day political interference, and demonstrably responded, no doubt influenced by its enthusiasm for India's independence, to the policies presented by the new governments in the states and at the Union. The political masters engaged in vast operations, consolidating India as a union of states, defining policy in the social and economic field, establishing a whole series of relationships between the states and the Union, and within each expressing parliamentary forms of procedure, regulation, and control for the governance of India. It was a time of variegated, comprehensive, carefully directed effort to establish and consolidate a popularly directed administrative system, to start institutions for economic and other purposes, and to define and embark on all-round plans of economic development.

Processes of a change from this situation were manifest in the period 1957 to 1966. The second general election of 1957 had apparently provided time enough for the political forces, expressed now through the universal adult vote, to discover new alignments of strength and organization in the electorate. A new type of politician began to appear in the state legislatures, and even to an extent in parliament. He was more nearly representative of the mass of the voters in objectives and character. He was less aware of the liberal tradition and ways. Evidence of this in the Punjab was the resounding confirmation of Partap Singh Kairon as Chief Minister by the election of an overwhelming majority of his 'men' to the state legislature. There were similar manifestations in other parts of India. Nevertheless, the trend and temper of administrative procedures remained substantially within the terms of the previous period. There were strains and difficulties such as those I have described in the Punjab (Chapter 7). The influence of Jawaharlal Nehru on the Congress Party was among the causes which contributed to continuity. The new forces that emerged were contained and indeed often provided stimulus to greater speed and experimentation with development. Though under severe strain, Nehru's influence even stood up to the Chinese debacle of 1962, and these methods were continued, in his short tenure as Prime Minister, by his successor, Lal Bahadur Shastri (1964–66). A marked feature common to both periods was that the leadership manifestly considered it their business to lead the administration and the people. With the help of the civil service, technical and general, they selected the programmes for action and put these persuasively to the people for acceptance and to the administration for implementation. Several controversial issues came up, particularly tricky those relating to language and the reorganization of states. Several compromises were made but these were controlled and directed by a continuously consolidated political will.

In the period after 1966 there are indications, growing more deep and intricate as each year passes, of the erosion of most of the fundamental administrative practices consolidated during the years after independence. These changes are possibly too near us, and their manifestations not fully worked out, to assess the results that might emerge. Some symptoms of what appears a deep and worsening malaise, which might indeed produce drastic results, can only be described. Whatever the forces at work, whether personal in the grim struggle for power and the split in 1969 within the Congress Party, or economic, social, or institutional, the fact seems clear that the political will no longer formulates and directs the decision-making process in terms of policy; instead it simply orders the administration to action in various situations. It appears to rouse and then wait on populist urges and seeks thereafter to square the policy account within the terms of immediate practical possibilities and limitations. It is difficult to say whether the people are no longer willing to accept the policy formulation of their elected leaders, or whether the latter, involved in the struggle for consolidating and keeping power, are no longer willing to accept the responsibility for this formulation, which necessarily involves, in India's circumstances, both restraint and discipline as well as sizeable compromises. It is perhaps not entirely coincidental that the Five-Year Plans were abandoned in 1966, followed by three *ad hoc* annual plans, and thereafter the return to the five-year system has been notional rather than actual. The result is a political and administrative system under continuous strain, adopting *ad hoc* and frequently unsuccessful remedies to a procession of deeper, more intricate, and apparently less easily alleviated, crises. The administrative system today, almost throughout India, is unsteady, at times and places even anarchical, its efficiency and objectivity generally assessed as being the lowest since independence. In this situation all the fundamental assumptions of order and administrative practice tend to be questioned and subject to continual cumulative erosion. The future of the whole administrative structure is at stake and it is by no means clear what answer will emerge. In particular, will India continue with, as it had succeeded in establishing, an administrative system built on the British model, where the civil services are substantially insulated and protected in implementing the policy of the government in power, or will it move to an arrangement where they are the creatures of and substantially indistinguishable from the party itself? With this question are also connected possible changes in the constitutional and political structure.

Another factor of overriding importance which has influenced the administration since independence is the vast increase in government interests and activities. The British administration in India governed too little and did not concern itself enough with changes in the social and economic order. Perhaps the Indian governments have governed too much. This may well have been inevitable, part of the temper of the times, since India gained independence when the idea of the welfare state was the generally accepted norm. India had also a great deal to make up to come abreast with other nations of the world. Government has certainly expanded its work in every conceivable direction from the arts and culture at one end to family planning at the other. Huge organizations for economic control, production and distribution have been established in both the Union and the states. Today government mandate crucially influences the supply of most essential services and products used by even the mass of people. Fertilizers, food, power, transport, irrigation, steel, cement, and bricks are only some of the commodities affected by government management or control. Where the life of the community, or at least its vital growth and development, depends so heavily on the administrative machine, any inefficiency or erosion in standards has a snowballing influence and gathers speed in geometric progression. India has indeed been caught up in the problem of governing less but effectively, or taking on more ineffectively. Each difficulty, whether economic or social, has tended to produce more rather than less government but the country has by no means turned the corner towards ensuring reasonable standards of prolonged good management.

Along with the expansion of government has inevitably gone an increase in bureaucracy particularly at the lower levels of organization. In fact in a country that cannot afford unemployment insurance, the creation of lower posts has often been used, especially at the state level, as some sort of substitute. This has contributed, along with other causes, to cynicism about and disenchantment with the public services, which have added to discontent and dissatisfaction. In turn there has been a lack of confidence and buoyancy in the services themselves.

Some observations on the nature of administration appear relevant. Administrative action, particularly in controversial matters, is something of a leap in the dark. Policy decides what is to be chosen as the objectives and how the wherewithal to implement these will be provided. The executive attempts to achieve these policies.* As most administrative action involves people and their interests, the executive is often acting in a situation which is developing and changing even as he makes decisions and goes ahead with achieving them. The point may best be illustrated by the extreme though simple example of a riot situation which the executive is called on to control, if necessary by the use of force. At the point of decision, for example whether or not to shoot, the executive cannot have all the facts, for these are developing even as he is deciding. At some stage he has to do the best he can on the best information he has. He takes the leap, in at least partial darkness, and commits himself to action which may well limit his options for the future. There is an element of this type of situation in most administrative action which depends, in the last analysis, on the judgement of the administrator, at whatever level of command the operative decisions are made. Administration is not, at the final count, a science nor can it be. It is an art. It only partakes somewhat, and the more the better, of the scientific.

In executive situations the operative acts must be decided on by individuals on their own responsibility within the powers and directives of policy. They cannot continuously be the subject of direction by discussion or other means without impeding their thrust and impairing and dividing responsibility. A degree of independence, within his sphere, must be allowed to the official to ensure efficient, responsible, and accountable action.

This does not mean that the actions of the executive are immune *post facto* to questioning, investigation, debate, and even reprimand. Nor that, before the event, they are not subject to decision, discussion, review, and revision with reference to the objectives he is to pursue and even to the conditions he is to fulfil in doing so. It does mean, however, a degree of immunity, of freedom of action, of essential judgement in

---

* The term 'executive' is used in this book in the sense commonly understood in administrative circles in India, to indicate those, usually officials, charged with actual performance and implementation of policy. Exceptions to this are references distinguishing the executive as a whole from the judiciary. The term 'administration', on the other hand, is used in the wider sense to include all those concerned with government, including ministers and policy-makers, but excluding the judiciary and the legislature.

the act of implementation. To perform correctly, he must enjoy limited but definite insulation from interference.

In authoritarian regimes this problem of executive insulation is presumably not as delicate or as difficult to solve as it is in democratic systems. The executive has the trust of the autocrat relevant to his duties; he acts with freedom, though perhaps more readily with excess than if he was responsible to a free public opinion. The sanction determining his conduct is removal, or at times and places even liquidation.

In a democratic regime it is usually the accretions of experience of the community and its leaders which progressively create accumulations of subjects and arenas where the executive is left unhampered to render service, whether preventive or even coercive as with the police, or positive and benevolent as with the health service. The executive knows that he may well be questioned if things go wrong, or investigated for undue favour. But cumulatively, progressively, and even in large areas of government, it is taken for granted—always subject to adequate performance—that activities are what may be termed 'routine administration'; they proceed unimpeded, taking their style almost instinctively from the temper of public opinion about them. It is in areas over and above this level that matters are delicate, that debate and disagreement are normal practice, that there are large elements of experimentation, of trial and error. Even in these delicate areas, once policy has been decided the executive often has his mandate and his protection for insulated action.

In the new democracy of India his has been a sphere of grave and recurring difficulty. The accumulated accretions of 'routine administration' have been small, with the result that where a powerful political personality, or difficult events, or other comparable reasons, produce a challenge, the whole sphere of administration gets charged with politics. Even fundamental matters, like dealing with crime, or with ration cards, taken very much for granted in the textbooks, may enter the area of debate, discussion, negotiation, with the use of any of the many weapons and inducements of the political game. In periods of stress and strain, too much administration at too ordinary a level, yet a level that influences and affects too many citizens, may well be politicized. The very body of the political and constitutional system and its administration shivers and shakes. India has been, and still is, deeply involved in creating and consolidating the minimum essential core of relationships and experience, in politics and administration, that are the foundations of democracy.

Nevertheless, for over twenty-five years India has sustained a working democracy in circumstances of enormous difficulty when many if not most other post-colonial new states have succumbed to various kinds of autocratic government. This democracy has maintained freedom, achieved development to a strong industrial base and an increase in food production, achieved a manifest though inadequate all-round increase in education and even prosperity, and maintained unity. It is today without doubt passing through a heightened crisis when all these and other issues seem at stake. In spite of this India's administration hopefully still has a destiny to achieve. The Occident tends to believe, indeed to proclaim, that democracy is a Western culture practice. India has provided the hope that democracy may well also be, at least, an eccentricity of the Orient.

2

BRITISH ADMINISTRATION IN THE PUNJAB, 1938–1947

The main executive in the British administrative system was the district officer. A description of the context of his work in the Punjab and the way his powers were exercised and sustained is useful to an understanding of the base from which post-independence administration started. The Punjab before independence had a population of 28.4 millions divided into twenty-nine districts. Lahore district had a population of 1.7 million, the largest in the province, explained by the size of its biggest city, the capital, with a population of nearly 700,000 in 1947. At the other extreme was Simla district, primarily an administrative centre, used as a summer capital by the governments of both India and Punjab. Its population was 39,000 in winter but liable to almost double itself during the peak summer season. Generally the size of a Punjab district was below one million. These were mostly compact areas easily accessible from the district headquarters. The two main exceptions were the Kangra district in the hills, the largest in area, and the Dera Ghazi Khan district. Kangra's 9,979 square miles was mostly valleys and mountains, some of the latter well over 20,000 feet, which made communication, much of it on foot or by animal, slow. In winter outlying areas, particularly the Lahaul and Spiti valleys which were entered over the Rohtang Pass (13,000 feet), were entirely closed to traffic. Dera Ghazi Khan was less forbidding and the problem here was access to the rest of the Punjab, involving a tiresome time-consuming crossing of the River Indus.

There were also variations in the culture and values of the people, particularly in religion, which eventually became the basis of a partition of the province. The religions enumerated by the 1941 census, the last before independence, were:

	million
Muslims	16.20
Hindus	7.50
Sikhs	3.70
Others	1.00

Almost every district shared the religious mix, though the Muslim population was more concentrated in the West, the Hindu and Sikh in the East. There was no 'pure' district from the point of view of religion or ethnic origin.

There was, however, one dominant theme in this diversity. That was the village, where the overwhelming bulk of the people lived, and which determined their social and economic life. The urban population was 4.36 million. This included many small towns inextricably connected to village ways of living. The Punjab had few large cities. The second biggest was Amritsar, with a population under 400,000, and there were five others which exceeded 100,000.

The way of life in the village was determined in its economic aspects by the relationship of the citizen to the land and was otherwise dominated by tradition, whose important ingredients were religion, caste, and family. There were forces making for change but by the time the British left in 1947 these had not made any marked impact. There were for example the 'canal colonies' comprising districts like Lyallpur, Montgomery, Sheikupura, and Jhang, where one of the finest irrigation systems in the world had introduced not only the occasion for new populations, 'settled' in them from other parts of the Punjab, but improved opportunities for economic development and mobility. Indeed these conditions were even referred to as producing the 'new Punjab'.

Moreover in the 1930s low import prices and general availability of trucks and buses had greatly extended their use for travel. Buses operated even in the interior on dirt tracks between villages and towns. The main urban centres were mostly served by tarmac roads, for which the Punjab enjoyed an enviable reputation.

Nevertheless the overwhelming mass of the population were confined for economic needs and the daily business of living to the ways of the village. Here the owner of land was the first recipient of its favours. But he was closely knit for his security, sense of belonging, even his labour and services, to other members of the community. Relationships were determined on the accumulated experience and tradition of the village. Even in 1947 payments were made almost entirely in kind, in the form of determined units of the crop at each harvest. The economic obligations between various members of the village were defined in the 'record of rights' at each Revenue Settlement, and could be enforced in the courts. Their essential sanction, however, was the will of the community, which gave them the quality and strength of social cement. While the landlord undoubtedly had the upper hand, his welfare was so interdependent with the rest of the village that the economically weak were regarded as a vested interest, their goodwill an investment for future generations, and their past performance a well-used cushion of security.

The village was also the conscience of the community. It was tyrannical and even oppressive when there was eccentricity or deviation. In important social matters such as birth, death, and marriage it enforced the dominant and traditional morality. Part of its creed was each man to his place and, provided this rule was kept both in work and socially, it conferred a degree of security, self-respect, and comfort on each of its inhabitants, including the underprivileged.

Similar processes determined the freedoms and rights of women. They were by no means relegated to the position of superior domestic servants of the family. They were indeed an integral part of the economic process. The woman not only cooked and brought up the children; she performed a variety of functions. She brought the midday meal to the fields, ministered to the many processes involved in the use of milk, often collected fuel or made cow-dung cakes for it, and looked after the cattle. Her position and influence was determined and respected by virtue of the needs she met. She often had a considerable voice in the family's decisions. Among the more prosperous who could afford to buy the services she performed, women tended to enjoy less freedom. They were indeed even physically secluded, behind the veil (*purdah*), among the more affluent Muslim families.

The village was not a wholly closed society. The need for credit for the community drove it to contacts with the money-lender. This was again a traditional relationship and generations of village folk had dealt with generations of money-lenders, sometimes living in the village but most often in the nearest market town, where the village took its surplus grain for disposal. The money-lender was usually a commission agent at this market and sold the grain for his client, providing ancillary services, like shelter overnight for both the farmer and his bullocks that pulled the grain carts to market. The money-lender would often recover his debt on selling the grain. For the big landlords he would even maintain a running account, a kind of safety and banking system. He no doubt used some of their money for his business and did not pay interest on it. In the 1930s the rate of interest charged by him was one pice per rupee per month, or 19 per cent per annum. Lending was seldom for a full year but rotated with the crop. In the event of crop failure, or a spate of social spending, the amounts and periods were extended and the rate of interest might well vary also. The whole system was personal, based on long and intimate knowledge. Its efficiency and resilience were remarkable. In its details particularly at times of economic stress the advantages lay with the money-lender. He was usually an outsider to the village, in the Punjab almost invariably a Hindu, and thus often of a different religion from most of the villagers. These considerations may have reduced the burden of his exactions when his clients were in distress, for his business, even his security, depended on long-term goodwill.

A strong sentiment against money-lending in the 1930s had led to the passage of what the urban community termed 'the black-bills', which sought to regulate the business and particularly to prevent the alienation of land to 'non-agricultural' classes. Sir Chhotu Ram, the Minister for Development, and later Revenue, in the late 1930s and early 1940s, was the chief protagonist of this reform. It is doubtful, however, whether money-lending declined in practice; indeed there was no efficient substitute to provide timely credit to the village, even for many years following independence.

Money-lending played a crucial role in the agricultural production of the Punjab and also helped in the marketing and distribution of the large wheat surplus, which was mostly routed through the wholesale trade, many of whose members were also money-lenders. The reputation and efficiency of the Punjab wholesaler, for both price and quality in the marketing of agricultural surpluses from the state, were held in high esteem among clients throughout the country.

Another need that drove the village community outwards was employment and, connected with it, education. There was no insistent universal demand for education. Opportunity was also limited. A primary school would be within walking distance of most villages; secondary and high schools might often be located only at the *tehsil* headquarters, a town in the sub-division of the district, comprising some 300 to 400 villages. Colleges were confined to the bigger towns. Girls' education, particularly in the hill areas and among Muslims, was largely neglected, and district officers often urged villagers to send their girls to schools where these existed.

The demand for work in the town, often described by the term 'service', was universal. The more wealthy landlord considered it a point of honour and a source of influence for the family if at least one of the sons was a civil or military officer. He would even send his sons to college at Lahore. Lower down there would be variations on this theme and ambition. In the great majority of the villages however some other avenue of work for one or more members of the family was sought to supplement income. In the poorer districts, dependent on rainfall for irrigation, it was also a much needed insurance against chancy production.

Opportunities for the employment of sizeable numbers were scarce. There was little industry in the Punjab and that limited to a few areas. A prestigious and much coveted position was in the army, which recruited substantial personnel from this province. Policy however tended to restrict recruitment to particular districts and groups. Thus the 'Punjabi Musalman' was recruited mostly from the districts of Rawalpindi, Jhelum, Mianwali, and Rajputs from Rohtak; the Sikh from the *doaba* (between the rivers Beas and Sutlej); the Haryana Jat from Rohtak; and the Dogra from Kangra and the adjoining Jammu region. Domestic service was another source of work; many of the 'bearers' of the *sahibs*, both white and brown, and in the army messes, hailed from the villages. The habit of 'service', particularly in the army, produced an injection of modern practices into the village through retired personnel and those who returned regularly on leave. For example, the soldier insisted on visiting hospital when he was ill and was disinclined to accept disease as an act of God, which was the more common attitude, confirmed by a situation where medical facilities were by no means adequate.

Throughout rural Punjab, with the exception of the hills, the idea of the Jat was important. The Jats were found among all the religions, Hindus, Muslims, and Sikhs, and it is difficult to characterize them by caste. The Jat tradition primarily involved a continuous association with farming and soldiering. The Jat thought of himself as special, an honest, down-to-earth man, a worker on the land, and a disciplined soldier, in contrast to the wily and complicated townsman, as also to the priests, shopkeepers, and wielders of pens. It was at least partly round the Jat sentiment that the Zamindara (also called 'Unionist') Party was built. This party was elected to power in 1937 following the 1935 Government of India Act, and, in spite of a weaker position in subsequent elections, was in political charge of the Punjab until 1947, when the decision for Partition swept it to oblivion.

The electorate was limited chiefly by property and educational qualifications, with some special provisions, however, for the weaker sections of society like Harijans and women. Constituencies were 'communal' and this meant not only that a number of seats was reserved for the main religions but that voters only voted in the particular constituencies reserved for their community. The Zamindara Party included all religions—Muslims who were 56 per cent of the population, Hindus, Sikhs, and Christians. It stood for the agricultural interest, landowners, tenants, and workers. The word *Zamindara* derives from *zamin*, meaning land. The most fiery and passionate politician in the party was Rao Bahadur Choudhry (later Sir) Chhotu Ram, landowner and lawyer of the Rohtak district. He proclaimed that he was there to protect, help and promote the Jat who he alleged had been exploited by the 'urbanites', particularly the money-lenders.

The Prime Minister, as the head of the provincial cabinet was then called, was in 1937 Sir Sikandar Hayat Khan, a big landowner of Wah in the Attock district. He had long experience of public affairs under the British. He was succeeded at his death in December 1942 by Nawab (later Sir) Khizar Hayat Khan Tiwana, of the Sargodha (Shahpur) district. The Tiwana family owned the largest landed estate in the region and were well-known for their tradition of hospitality, sport, and cosmopolitan sociability, which brought them friends from all the communities and from the British.

Other persons who were members of the cabinet at one time or another during this period were Sir Manohar Lal, the Finance Minister, elected by the University, a highly suave and practical economist, whose interests were largely confined to the drawing-room and the desk; Baldev Singh, himself a Jat, and both landowner (in the Punjab) and industrialist (in Bihar) who later became India's first Defence Minister; Swaran Singh (later Home Minister in post-independence Indian Punjab and in recent years India's Foreign Minister) who was also a Jat and was chosen in preference to the better known Ujjal Singh.

Khizar Hayat Khan Tiwana was a man of rare excellence. Though not highly educated or sophisticated he had a capacity for friendship and qualities of discretion and persuasion which enabled him to administer the Punjab over four difficult war and pre-independence years (1943–7), with consummate and apparently unstrained skill.

The personnel of this government represented primarily the landed interests in the Punjab. It cut across religious divisions and firmly ignored these in policy. Nevertheless it recognized the pattern of the communities. Thus by convention the Prime Minister was always a Muslim; half his cabinet was drawn from that community and the other half divided in a two to one ratio between Hindus and Sikhs. Most members of the government had a long tradition of work with the British regime. Sikandar Hayat Khan had even acted as Governor on two occasions between regular appointments. Khizar Hayat had been a captain in the army. His father, General Sir Umar Hayat Khan Tiwana, had been an honorary staff officer to the King. Many of the cabinet had been knighted. With such credentials from the past this government operated a continuity in the systems and procedures of the administration, with whose day to day work they did not interfere. There was no suspicion on their part of the civil service. They concerned themselves primarily with changes in law to enforce their policy. The 'black bills' to control money-lenders have already been mentioned; another significant effort was in the direction of strengthening the administration of *panchayats* (village councils) and the cooperative movement, especially in the form of credit societies.

The Punjab was an exception to developments elsewhere in India, where the first elected provincial governments under the Act of 1935, seven out of eleven from Congress, had brought the opposition to British rule squarely into power and where the struggle for greater autonomy was part of their daily business. It would, however, be wrong to assume that the Zamindara government was merely a 'yesman' of the British. It had emerged in the process of politics and history in the Punjab and was a pragmatic, workable compromise of the interests that operated in the province. It represented continuity in administrative method but pursued a defined policy in this context. Khizar Hayat Khan in 1945 appointed the first Indian Chief Secretary of the Punjab, and a little later the first Indian Deputy Inspector-General of Police to the Criminal Investigation Department, the top intelligence agency. It was not entirely accident that both these officers were Christians, thus avoiding a selection from, and the mutual suspicion of, the two major religions.

It was against this broad background that the district officer performed his trinity of functions as 'collector', 'district magistrate' and 'deputy commissioner', representing respectively the head of the revenue agency, that of law and order, and the chief executive. I do not propose to describe these functions and their organization in detail but to underline the salient characteristics of the district officers' control of the administration.

In its land revenue organization the Punjab had established direct contact between the government and the persons actually concerned with the land, as owners, tenants, or workers. There were no intermediaries. This was achieved not only by law but by routine. The administration maintained for each crop a record indicating in each village how each field had been used; it also gave the names of the owner and other persons in any way associated with the cultivation.

The organization for these arrangements was at the base a group of villages, two to four, in charge of a village accountant (*patwari*). Above this there was the *tehsil*, with two officers, a *tehsildar* and his assistant, comprising usually three to four hundred villages; between the two there were itinerant inspectors to check the work. The *tehsil* was also a government treasury, the supervision of which was the responsibility of the collector, assisted by at least one whole-time officer of the provincial civil service, described as revenue assistant.

A similar organization working under an executive engineer irrigation (invariably called XEN) maintained a more detailed record of crops and waterings for canal irrigated land; on this basis were calculated the irrigation dues, the incidence of which was considerably higher than the land revenue. This organization also supervised the distribution of water to villages and between cultivators. As water vitally influenced the economics of these villages, this organization was in more intense day to day touch with cultivators and an object of grave concern to them. The collector was in overall supervision of the XEN irrigation as far as his district went and the superior forum of appeal or review in cases of dispute. Most of the work relating to irrigated land was however finally settled at or below the XEN's level. The irrigation organization functioned only where there were canals, a comparatively small, and mostly compact, area of the province.

The land revenue was fixed at a periodic settlement. The law provided that the interval between settlements should not exceed forty years. In the Punjab the general practice was an interval of thirty years, unless canal irrigation had been introduced, in which case the settlement was earlier. A settlement officer, an experienced collector, was appointed to the district for three to four years to make a thorough economic survey of each tract in it. The government then fixed the land revenue on the basis of his report.

The settlement officer was required to revise the 'Record of Rights' (called *Jamabandi*) for each village, indicating meticulously the ascertained claims of all interests in each ownership, and for the village generally the quantum of payments for each class of worker.

The settlement officer wrote, or revised, the *District Gazetteer*, a compendium of detailed information on all aspects of the district. These books are stores of accurate knowledge, some of them being also literary productions of merit.

The revenue organization was by no means merely a collector of government dues but also the repository of up-to-date knowledge and documentation of all the rights vested in land. Its much bigger function in the Punjab was as arbiter of disputes in regard to these. The law provided that each hierarchy of the revenue agency should determine within defined powers such rights in case of dispute. In this way levels of appeal and review existed right from the *tehsil*, through the collector and his immediate boss, the divisional commissioner, to the head of the revenue organization, the financial commissioner at the provincial capital. A final appeal on points of law lay from the financial commissioner's court to the High Court. A substantial body of law and precedents had been built up over the years.

This system had the strength and advantage that most of the decisions about land rights—relating comprehensively to ownership, tenancy, labour rights, and the like—were made by a hierarchy of officers who were in constant touch with their administration—and with the people —as executives. Procedures were quick and simple; knowledge in court was often refreshed, and even sought, by direct contact at the village itself with the people concerned.

The district officer in his second role as 'district magistrate' was charged with two main responsibilities. He was the direct superior of all the magistrates working in the district. Their number varied depending on the state of crime and law and order in the district. Magistrates were mostly located at headquarters but were also available in outlying parts. Each *tehsildar* was a second-class magistrate and his deputy, the *naib-tehsildar*, of the third class. The more important *tehsils* were also called 'sub-divisions' with a sub-divisional officer located in them. He was often a junior ICS officer under training to become a collector, and sometimes a senior officer of the provincial civil service.

The second responsibility of the district magistrate was that he was the head of the law and order agency in the district and thus in overall charge of the police. This was a delicate and difficult position. The police were under the command of a superintendent of police, himself a member of an all-India service, the Indian Police. The district magistrate had no direct disciplinary authority over the superintendent of police. Far from being able to hire or fire, he did not even report on his work as a police officer. Nevertheless the mandate of policy defined the district magistrate as the head of the law and order organization. In practice the two officers maintained the closest touch with each other; the superintendent of police was seldom interfered with in matters of ordinary crime but invariably acted under the supervision and guidance of the district magistrate where any political, agitational, or religious question was involved. The policy and practice of civil control of the police at the district level functioned and flourished basically on convention and the good sense and pragmatism of the two officers. It worked well. This relationship has been a subject of considerable strain in independent India.

Relations between the civil administration and the police were lubricated by the very fact of their interdependence which was built into the legal system and its procedures. If the police arrested a suspect he had to be produced before a magistrate for orders for his further detention or release. In a riot situation the presence of a magistrate was of assistance in declaring an assembly unlawful, ordering dispersal, and in extreme cases approving the use of force. As the magistracy worked directly under the district magistrate, and were his subordinates, his influence could be used to ensure that the police were supported when required. The police in turn responded to and often welcomed the requirement of civilian control.

As deputy commissioner the district officer was the executive, co-ordinating authority for all administrative matters on behalf of the government. It was in this capacity that his duties and powers had grown. The revenue agency and, in times of amity, law and order became matters of routine, whereas his duties as executive gained in variety and complexity. It is in this sphere that it is most difficult to attempt any kind of exhaustive list of his responsibilities.

He was in charge of the supervision of the local government institutions in the district. For rural areas this was the district board, of which the district commissioner was often chairman. Even where he was not chairman he was guide, counsellor, and friend. His defined powers permitted interference and even a degree of control. He exercised similar powers in regard to the municipalities.

The deputy commissioner was also associated with organizations like the Red Cross, soldiers, sailors and airmen boards, famine relief funds, sports promotion, and a variety of efforts of an ostensibly voluntary type, where the essential initiative rested with the government through personnel sponsored and helped by it. Even in societies run entirely by the public, of which there were several, usually inspired by religious motivation, including schools, colleges, and dispensaries, the deputy commissioner often had a role to play. The acquisition of a piece of land at a reasonable price, or the construction of an approach road could be problems where official help, attention, or goodwill were useful.

The deputy commissioner was the accepted coordinator of the activities of all the departments working in the district. There were several specialized units of government dealing for example with agriculture (through deputy and assistant directors), cooperatives (assistant registrars), buildings and roads (XENs), *panchayats*, and health, which had their own lines of command from provincial headquarters downwards. The deputy commissioner was not the superior of these hierarchies but it was expected that they would fall in line with and indeed assist him on any matter where joint effort was required and accept his as the deciding voice where any departmental interests clashed. Organizations not within the control of the provincial government, such as army authorities, accepted the district officer as the official representative of the local public and sought his assistance and guidance in matters where their requirements or actions had any public impact.

The deputy commissioner's authority was achieved partly by the fact that the government recognized him alone for this overall role and supported him in making it effective. He could often thereby provide the lubricants of influence and persuasion to achieve departmental success for the officers working under his jurisdiction. If for example the army recruiting officer wished to recognize the services of a non-official who had assisted in recruitment, by the grant of a title or a concession of land in a canal colony, the government would normally look at the proposal only after it had received the district officer's comments. It was accepted convention and tradition that government did not bless or approve unless the district officer had done so already.

Another source of strength to the district administration was the fact that at several levels it presented a multi-faceted and multi-powered authority. The deputy commissioner, his subordinate the sub-divisional officer, and below him the *tehsil* officers, empowered with revenue authority, also acted as magistrates and under various laws and dispensations as executive functionaries. The *tehsildar* in addition was in charge of the local treasury. The combination of several kinds of power in one person made for concentration of impact and manoeuvrability. One component of power was used, often by implication rather than definition, to support and utilize another. A deputy commissioner with reasonable qualities of leadership and intelligence could exercise in these ways considerable pressure to achieve his objectives in administration.

Magistrates at headquarters were also employed to assist the district officer in the administration of particular subjects. The work load was in fact divided among them. One would be in charge of local bodies, another of arms licences, a third of transport licences, and so on. The principle of multi-purpose functions applied in this way to most of the officer staff in the district.

The two clerical pillars of the deputy commissioner's office were the superintendent and the head vernacular clerk. They were also quite frequently men of great physical size—perhaps a result of sitting long hours at the desk or squatting, as the head vernacular clerk did, cross-legged on the floor.

The deputy commissioner's officer assistants at headquarters were magistrates and it was the business of the superintendent to keep the record for all branches of what was termed the 'English office'. He systematized, referenced, and prepared material for decisions and then conveyed these to the clients concerned. As a keeper of the record the superintendent's responsibility was secondary; orders had always to be passed by an officer or the deputy commissioner himself. The superintendent was nevertheless regarded by the public as a man of influence and great pains were taken to keep him in good humour. He could certainly delay a decision.

The head of the vernacular office, the head vernacular clerk, was regarded with greater suspicion. He dealt with all papers which came up and required orders in Urdu, the official language of the Punjab. Most of the work relating to land cases and thus concerning the vast number of citizens would be in Urdu. While every district officer was required to know Urdu, his proficiency in the written language was usually low. Written Urdu is a kind of shorthand called *shakasta* and is difficult, without regular practice, even for a person whose mother tongue it is. The result was that the head vernacular clerk almost invariably presented his cases to the deputy commissioner in what was termed *peshi* (that is, with his presence). He would sit crosslegged on the floor with a vast bundle of papers before him, while the deputy commissioner sat at a table, and gave his orders verbally. These would be recorded by the head vernacular clerk in Urdu and signed by the deputy commissioner. The public believed that this procedure gave the head vernacular clerk an opportunity to use his discretion to twist matters in favour of or against clients.

The system, even in spite of the ministrations of the head vernacular clerk, on the whole worked efficiently and with justice. An important reason for this was the administration's insistence that its officers, particularly those dealing with land subjects, should constantly tour. The horse thus played a pre-eminent role in official life. It was compulsory for a deputy commissioner and for many of his subordinates, including the *tehsildar* and the field inspectors, to maintain a horse. At the *tehsil* and lower levels allowances were provided on condition that a horse was kept. Rules prescribed the number of days and nights to be spent out on tour. Rest houses were provided at suitable distances for travel on horseback. The horse was indeed not only an instrument of administration, enabling officers to be the 'eyes and ears' of the government, but was also a cult; at the top levels of the hierarchy, where riding was not prescribed as obligatory, it was nevertheless encouraged by way of habit and example, an addiction and symbol of 'the service'.

The business of a touring officer in a village was to check and ensure that his department's work was promptly and adequately performed. He also reported to his superior if he noticed or heard of any matter of interest relating to other branches of government. If his superior thought fit he would send the information to the department concerned. A habit of continuously replenished information was in this way built up over the months and years and the deputy commissioner, placed as he was at the hub of the whole district system, could not for any length of time remain unaware of any significant trends in his jurisdiction. Supervising officers on tour frequently enquired into specific complaints in the village itself and within their powers redressed incorrect or malafide decisions.

The revenue organization came to be used as a 'maid of all work' by the government. Its tentacles spread in uniform structure throughout the province into each village. Any additional general item of work was apt to be thrust on it. Thus when there was the ten-year census the supervision of enumeration was most often made its responsibility. In times of strain, or when the government extended its interests to new work involving the mass of its citizens, the services of the revenue agency were almost invariably used.

Above the district there were two tiers of government for executive supervision, inspection, and the formulating and control of policy. These were at the division, comprising five to seven districts, and at the provincial headquarters, the secretariat, comprising the government, headed by the ministers and the Governor.

The head of the general administration at the division was the commissioner, the immediate superior of the deputy commissioners. His work comprised the executive supervision and inspection of the districts, which included considerable touring; he was the deciding statutory authority for several kinds of cases, appellate authority for others, including those relating to personnel, discipline, and punishment and a court of appeal from the collector in defined classes of land cases. Other departments of government also had an officer at the division to supervise their work; the police had a deputy inspector-general corresponding to the commissioner, the Public Works Department a superintending engineer.

At government headquarters at Lahore were the heads of departments, who were the executive chiefs of the administration; and the secretariat. Among these heads were the inspector-general of police, the inspector-general of hospitals (in charge of the Health Department), the registrar of cooperative societies and the director of agriculture. The Punjab system generally insisted that the function of head of department should be organized in a separate hierarchy from that of the secretariat. These were two distinct offices which corresponded formally with each other; that is, they did not work on the basis of a single file with noting between the officers of each. The war produced some exceptions. In 1943 a separate department of Food and Civil Supplies was created and, in the interests of speed for the sake of what seemed a temporary war need, this combined both top executive and secretariat operations in the same personnel at headquarters.

The secretariat, housed in a small complex of single-storeyed buildings which today would contain only a fraction of a post-independence state government, was strictly a policy-making body. The exception to this was that it was also the final administrative forum for review and appeal from decisions made in the field.

The Punjab secretariat had two parts. The 'financial commissioner's secretariat' dealt with land problems and rural development; and the 'civil secretariat' with all other subjects. The financial commissioners, of whom there were two, invariably from the ICS, were the most senior officers of the government: and they were the most highly paid civilian administrative officials in the provincial government; only a secretary to the Government of India in Delhi was paid more. This was apparently a means of establishing the idea that the government gave the highest priority to land problems which concerned the vast mass of the population. The financial commissioner's position was elevated in other ways too. He was encouraged to hold public *durbars* (meetings of some formality) and his tours were publicized. In common parlance he was referred to as the *chota lat sahib* (the smaller, or second, Governor).

The 'civil secretariat' was headed at administrative level by secretaries to government, about eight to ten in number, each in charge of a group of subjects. There were thus a home secretary, law secretary, education secretary, and so on. Each secretary worked directly under the minister for the subject, and was usually also in contact with the Governor. Most of the secretaries were from the ICS, the exceptions being those dealing with education and public works, although electricity engineering was usually attached to one of the ICS secretaries along with other subjects. Secretaries were in status and function equal and usually of similar experience to senior collectors; again the technical secretaries were often more senior in age, of the rank for example of chief engineer of the Public Works Department.

The only exception to this pattern was the chief secretary, who had overall coordinating functions for the government as a whole and who was of the rank of commissioner, senior in both emoluments and experience to a collector. The chief secretary controlled directly, for the province, the main administrative services: the ICS and the provincial civil service. He was also the coordinating supervisory authority for personnel generally. He was *ex officio* secretary to the Council of Ministers. He enjoyed overall powers in regard to all interdepartmental matters, and also where administration in any way touched on politics. In exercising the last responsibility he had access to confidential intelligence appreciations from districts and the intelligence organization of the CID (Criminal Investigation Department) at headquarters working under the inspector-general of police and home secretary.

The chief secretary thus in a variety of ways functioned as the administrative head of the civil service and the coordinating head of the policy-making process. The British regime however insisted that this officer should be junior in experience, pay, and status to the financial commissioner. This arrangement provided manoeuvrability; the chief secretary could be selected from one of half a dozen officers of commissioner's rank, thus giving the government a wider range of choice to secure the appropriate person. Moreover, he was constantly aware of working at headquarters close to the financial commissioners more senior than himself; this induced moderation and care in the exercise of considerable powers that intimately concerned the services and their morale.

Civilian control of the police was repeated on the model of the district in the relationship between the home secretary and the inspector-general of police, except that the former was by definition in superior administrative control of the police department. The home secretary enjoyed a strong position in the government. He was in intimate touch with intelligence through the inspector-general and deputy inspector-general of police and sought guidance more than his colleagues by direct and frequent contact with the Governor. He had dossiers about the main political parties and characters in the province and, when occasion demanded, was able at short notice to take action against those engaged in agitation or in planning violence against the government. The Punjab before independence never appointed an Indian officer as home secretary, perhaps an indication of the security significance attached to this position.

Another instrument of special power in the hands of the police for the purpose of dealing with emergencies was the arrangement that the inspector-general was *ex officio* a joint secretary to the government and thereby entitled to issue orders carrying the highest sanction of the law. In practice these powers were used only in cases of urgency or for the purpose of simplifying procedures.

Generally the secretaries were provided with little officer support for their work was confined rather strictly to policy and coordination. In principle, below a secretary were, in order, deputy secretary, under secretary, and assistant secretary, the first two of these being officers serving in the executive and posted to the secretariat for varying periods, while the assistant secretary was a member of the secretariat office staff who had come up through the ranks. However, prior to the war in the Punjab there were only two posts of under secretaries and one of deputy secretary in the whole government. At times a special short-term position would be created to meet a special need, for example to deal with famine.

The office staff was organized in sections, headed by a superintendent, a number of assistants (three to five), two to three clerks to keep the record, and peons. The peon tradition was strong. Secretaries usually each had two, the financial commissioner three. They rendered both official duties in fetching and distributing papers and marginally an amount of personal service to the officer and his family.

The war increased the number of officers at the secretariat and this increase was regarded at the time as a temporary phenomenon. In the Food and Civil Supplies department there were by 1946 at the head-quarters secretariat as many as nine ICS officers and about a dozen from the provincial civil service or equivalent services. Somewhat similar changes took place in the organizations for civil defence and transport.

The top policy-makers were the ministers and Governor. The cabinet of the time usually had six, never more than eight, ministers, including the Prime Minister. The cabinet as such met rarely, in contrast to the practice after independence. There was, however, frequent consultation between individual ministers and by each with the Prime Minister. Thus Baldev Singh, the Food and Civil Supplies minister, would usually consult Chhotu Ram, the revenue minister, on matters concerning controls affecting the farmer.

The Governor wielded both influence and power. Consultation between him and the secretaries was constant, sometimes in the presence of the appropriate minister, sometimes without. Both Sir Bertrand Glancy (1941–6) and Sir Evan Jenkins (1946–7) concerned themselves intimately with all the more crucial developments in policy and action. Jenkins would frequently want even to see and vet the draft of important letters before they were issued to the districts. In the Punjab, however, there was no friction between the ministry and the Governor regarding the use of influence and supervision by the latter. Generally ministers were in touch with him and their interests apparently did not conflict to the point of tension.

The conclusion seems justified that in the Punjab during this phase of the British period joint cabinet responsibility was not effectively the method of decision. The minister enjoyed considerable freedom, initiative, and patronage within his portfolio and exercised these in consultation with his more important colleagues and the Prime Minister. The Governor had a crucial voice in decisions on critical issues and in the overall supervision of performance.

The judiciary was substantially an independent organization but there was an intimate link in experience and personnel between it and the executive. The basic position in the judicial hierarchy was that of district and sessions judge, corresponding to the deputy commissioner and usually located at district headquarters. Several of the district judges were members of the ICS. An ICS officer was normally required to do two years' judicial service and training while in positions below collector or district judge and in preparation for appointment to either of these positions. He was also required to do eighteen months' executive training before he held even a junior independent post. The shortage of officers following the First World War, and the demand for them during the Second, usually prevented the completion of the full two years' judicial experience. All ICS officers, however, invariably did eighteen months' executive work. Thereafter those appointed to the executive tended to remain there. Interchange between the two wings was, however, always a recognized possibility, though in practice it became more difficult. A good proportion of the district judges were in fact ICS officers who had done at least a period of executive work. At that time the executive was generally rated higher than the judiciary and right down to the end of the British period officers of the judiciary often managed to get posted back to the executive.

Nor did the ICS officer finally assigned to the judiciary stop at the district judge's level. Members of the High Court were often selected from ICS district judges. Other sources of appointment were members of the Bar or legal personnel from the United Kingdom. The last source of recruitment had diminished but the chief justice of the Punjab was almost without exception a direct appointment from England. Even the last two chief justices, Sir Douglas Young (1938–42) and Sir Trevor Harries (1943–6) were selected in this way. In 1947, just before independence, an Indian, Sir Mian Abdul Rashid, was appointed. In fact on the selection of the English lawyer in 1943 one of the Indian members of the High Court, Justice Dalip Singh, had resigned in protest.

Civil jurisdiction not connected with the land revenue organization rested entirely with the judiciary, starting with the sub-judge, recruited to the provincial civil service (judicial branch), and going on through district judge to the High Court. However, criminal jurisdiction up to and including the district magistrate was vested in the executive; it was only above the district magistrate that jurisdiction and appeals lay to the district judge and the High Court. In land cases appeals on points of law went from the financial commissioner to the High Court. This vital link in experience and personnel between the executive and the judiciary strengthened both the impact of the total administration and the comprehension of its parts by the senior personnel of government.

Some description of the men who ran the administration is appropriate. The leadership of the system was squarely vested in the ICS, the famous 'steel frame'. This was recruited substantially by competitive examination in London and Delhi and the aim by this time was to have equal proportions of British and Indians. There was provision for the nomination of minorities, almost exclusively Muslims, usually selected within their group from their position in the competitive examination. In 1935 provision for the nomination of British personnel was also introduced to maintain numbers, though it was also stated that competition alone had failed to produce the right type of British officer. Cynics alleged that the economic depression had so increased the entry of grammar school boys into the imperial service that the British ruling class had been appalled!

ICS candidates usually needed to possess high-class degrees to enter the competition. They were thereafter initially trained at one of the great British universities—Oxford, Cambridge, London, or Trinity College Dublin—and once in service not only held the key administrative posts but rose to high and expanding responsibilities at a comparatively young age. In the Punjab an officer attained collector's rank usually within six to eight years and when there was a shortage of officers even within three to four. Only 15 per cent of the senior administrative posts could go to promoted officers of the provincial civil service. They achieved these a few years before retirement as a reward for good work rather than as an opportunity for a future career. The ICS also manned the administrative positions in the central government. Interchange between district, provincial headquarters, and the Delhi government was constant and an ICS officer was rarely allowed to become a specialist. A good 75 per cent of the prestigious positions, such as those of Governors, outside and usually above the main administrative stream, were held by the ICS. All the Governors of the Punjab during this period were from the ICS except for one or two short-term acting appointments. The ICS also had opportunity for high responsibility in the judiciary. They were thus in crucial, almost exclusive, command of all branches of the administration.

Below the ICS was the provincial civil service recruited partly by competition and partly by nomination. The latter method was used to ensure the representation of the various communities. The Punjab formula was 50 per cent for Muslims, 15 per cent for Sikhs, and the balance for Hindus and others. Nomination was also useful to secure the entry of educated men from the landed and other interests and as an avenue of promotion from the lower services. A detailed set of rules for recommendations for nomination was prescribed and ample opportunity was permitted to district officers to push the claims of men working under them or citizens of their districts. The final selection was made in consultation between the Public Service Commission and the provincial government. Entry into the Public Service Commission was a spur to the ambition of many of the leading families who often educated their sons in this hope at the government, or the Forman Christian, colleges at Lahore, assessed as the leading degree institutions, and carrying with them the seal of good sportsmanship, the marks of 'the gentleman', and even a degree of intellectual prowess.

The Indian Police which was the other 'all-India service', also comprising British and Indians in equal numbers, was recruited in a similar manner to the ICS but was trained entirely in India. The specialized services—engineers, doctors, educationalists, agricultural personnel, etc.—were by the 1930s recruited almost exclusively in India. British officers were brought in on the basis of selective appointments for a proportion of the senior supervisory posts.

In all departments centralized recruiting ceased below the pay scale of Rs 250-750. Those posts in this scale and above it which were recruited by the provincial government were in the charge of the Public Service Commission, but lower posts—junior officers, inspectors, clerks, etc.—were recruited on a decentralized basis of selection by departments. In this way local executive officers had a considerable voice in the exercise of patronage through appointments and promotions in their organizations.

In general, however, these arrangements were not worked in a manner which gave an impression of arbitrary selection. Even where nominations were permitted, or selections by promotion based on the recommendation of executives, the whole procedure was reduced to a known set of rules. Often the discretion was exercised less to favour for than to exclude from appointment. On the other hand the system was elastic and offered scope for the reward of good service within government, as well as for political and public service outside.

Patronage was also available, again substantially to district officers, through the selection of non-official personnel to aid the administration.

There were for example the appointments of village headmen; apart from rendering general assistance to the government, particularly the police, they collected the land revenue and were paid one-fifth of it as fee. This might amount to a nominal sum in many villages, but the position was coveted and on occasion became the subject of litigation which went up to the financial commissioner and even to the High Court. There were also other rural non-official, and mostly entirely unpaid, positions variously described, the most commonly known in the Punjab being the *sufed posh* (literally 'clothed in white'—that is, respectable) and the *zaildar* (the notable of a *zail*, a Mughal term meaning thirty to fifty villages). These men had no precise responsibilities. They acted as general assistants to the administration, informants to the police, helpers in locating witnesses and getting them to stick to their evidence, looked after touring officers and rendered sundry services of this type. In return they secured accessibility to the officials in power, *tehsildars*, sub-inspectors of police, and above all the collector. There was in this way a large class of busybodies and influence-seekers—some of whom never achieved any place or recognition—who produced an atmosphere of flattery and subservience which was a marked feature of administrative public relations.

The British system did not provide separate, specialized organizations for watching and eliminating corruption in the services. This responsibility was squarely placed on the supervisory officers in the departments, particularly the executive head. 'Tipping' was an almost universal custom—a little money paid for an interview, a document, or the like—but usually this did not go so far as to make the availability of a decision dependent on graft. Officials living in or close to villages undoubtedly received presents in kind for their domestic needs, wheat in season, fodder for a horse, *ghee* (clarified butter) for cooking, wood in forest areas. At the higher levels of government, that is the district officer and above, the administration had a high reputation for honesty. This indeed was so dominant a theme at the time that in the few cases where an officer was suspected as corrupt, his reputation spread so quickly through the province that even before he arrived at a new posting his price was known in the bazaars. He was already watched, a marked man.

These assessments require some qualification in regard to the police and public works. The police were generally considered tough and were recognized as dealing with equally tough criminals and *goondas* (professional thugs). Their methods matched this material. They were widely believed to extract benefits for themselves. They were assessed, possibly with truth, as both efficient and corrupt. That some of the corruption went beyond the proportions of tipping, and even infected a minority of their senior level officers, there seems little doubt.

In the Public Works Department there was persistent belief that the hierarchies, even at the district level, and sometimes right up to and including the chief engineers, practised what was called 'percentage'. This meant that a fixed proportion of each bill paid to a contractor for works was distributed among the staff dealing with the contract, in known quantities, all along the line. The war brought a spate of urgent works and the prevalent scarcity of essential raw materials increased the temptations and opportunity for corruption. The situation did not however assume proportions of scandal nor of inefficiency; indeed there can be no certainty as to how far corruption was practised.

The strength of the British administrative system in the Punjab was its high degree of integration. This was brought about by organizational arrangements which were concentrated at and dependent upon the district officer. Supervision, coordination, and control merged and operated in his person, and the *firman* (the order) of policy and action, of information and correction ran from Delhi, through the province, to the district and village. This process was assisted by hierarchical arrangements which cemented service personnel in experience by rotation within the system. At leadership level they felt the same way, at least partly because they had all been exposed to varying experience in the crucial parts of the system. Personnel were interchanged within the line of command, and even, as in the judiciary, outside it in allied or related functions. The circumstance and history of British rule also created, built, and sustained the spirit of the club, a kind of conspiracy and administrative mission to rule.

There seems little truth in the accusation that the administration at its higher levels was in the hands of its minions and subject to environmental pressures. It is true that it was thinly spread, particularly the British officers. On the other hand accumulations and accretions of the system over the decades, its constant insistence on touring and the use of the horse, the adamant and detailed priority given to knowledge of the agricultural interests—cultivator, owner, tenant, and labourer, ensured that district officers were highly knowledgeable. Indeed the officers of the Punjab knew the rural people intimately and were in effective control of their governance. It is possibly appropriate to mention that the Punjab was reputed to have the ablest among the ICS, though this may well be a cultivated myth.

Where the administration lacked knowledge, or at least access, was with the Indian middle class intelligentsia, politically aware and either openly non-cooperative or, the majority, sullenly acquiescent. This middle class had progressively, and almost finally, become a separate world—outsiders without a bridge. The necessities of the revenue system were not their need. No other bridge had been evolved where minds, or even needs, might meet.

This was a *status quo* regime. It maintained and preserved broadly the structure of rural society as it found it. It prevented exploitation by codifying rights, making them generally known and available, and manifestly maintaining them by a simple and quick system of ventilation, enquiry, and decision. The administration redressed glaring inequity such as that created by famine. It did not concern itself with radical, or even specific, change. It was not a prompter, or arbiter, for economic and social reform. Even efforts associated with the campaign of F. L. Brayne for the betterment of village life were largely confined to inducing habits of hygiene, better production, and more orderly relations within the known dimensions of the social and economic structure. The impact of the administration on the vast bulk of citizens was minimal, like the sky overhead. They 'encountered' it only if they rebelled or revolted, or committed crimes. Perhaps the only exception to this was the canal irrigated areas where the distribution and costs of water produced more constant, and conscious, meeting of men and problems. Nor were ideas of radical social change part of the climate of the time. Even stalwart nationalists, like Motilal Nehru and Gandhi, suspected and opposed socialism.

The more relevant question is whether the administration prepared for its meeting with destiny within the terms of its own credentials. Did it plan, as was its defined objective, from as early as the 1920s for a crucial transfer of power to the hands of Indians? There are few indications that it did and perhaps no one was taken by greater surprise than the Punjab administration when power was in fact transferred in 1947.

More significant, and more controversial, is the attitude of the administration to the religious question. In the Punjab the government had provided peace and a context in which the people had achieved amity, constructive competition, and a cooperative detente between the religions. This was expressed and reflected in an active political party, including all the faiths, which had been in power since the 1937 elections. Yet the administration worked on the assumption, often given institutional basis, of a schism between the major religions. Could a different administrative approach, tilted in favour of unity, have changed the balance of forces and events that swept unity aside and brought about partition? On another great, potentially divisive issue, that concerning 'the princes', the 'tilt' finally administered by the British Raj was towards unity, with vastly different results.

3

FOOD ADMINISTRATION, 1942–1950

In terms of the needs of consumers, food in India means the basic cereals. These were the main subject of the government's controls following the war and this chapter deals almost exclusively with them. Rice and wheat, the 'major cereals', are the most important. Rice is the food of roughly two-thirds of the population, wheat of one-third. The 'minor cereals' which include barley, *jawar*, maize, *bajra*, and gram have a marked influence on the availability and price of the major cereals, and any regulatory system must be concerned with them as a necessary aid to the control of wheat and rice.

Generally northwest India is wheat-consuming and the rest rice-eating, but this distinction cannot be made rigidly. Bigger towns have mixed populations. On ceremonial and social occasions rice is rated highly. In the north it is served in many varieties of *pilau*, and at weddings, frequently decked with colour and garnishings with as great care as the bride herself. During the war wheat had often to substitute for rice, as it could be imported more easily and cheaply from world markets. The loss of Burma by the British in 1942 eliminated a source of supply of about one million tons of rice a year. Much of the labour cultivating rice there had been provided by seasonal migration from India: this labour received at least part of their remuneration in rice, which they brought home.

Food controls have been a problem tackled for the entire country, even though much of the detailed administration has been provincial. There are wide variations in production in relation to local needs. The Punjab, known at the time as 'the granary of India', was in 1939 the biggest supplier of wheat in the country; it provided some rice too and the largest surplus of gram when rain was plentiful. Gram was a notoriously chancy crop, grown almost exclusively in rain-fed areas, of significant use for human diet, but of crucial importance as an animal feed, particularly for milch cattle and horses. On the other hand the province of Bombay, with its huge urban industrial population, was a perennially deficit area, dependent on other provinces for wheat, rice, and even minor cereals. The regulation of food has thus never been planned or administered as a problem of the province (later state) but always at an all-India level.

At the start of the war prices were phenomenally low following the slump. Wheat was selling at Lyallpur, the Punjab's biggest surplus district, at Rs 2 annas 8 per maund (less than 20p for 82 lb). Other prices were also low; it was a veritable consumers' paradise. There was general relief, in the Punjab particularly, that agricultural prices were rising. In some other provinces, notably the deficit ones of Bombay and Madras, on the other hand, there was apprehension and preliminary plans were made, at a local level, to introduce degrees of regulation should this become necessary. In fact the pioneering experiments and effort of these provinces, particularly Bombay, blazed the trail for the more effective and scientific methods of control that events soon made inevitable.

The Government of India's initial provision to meet possible difficulties was to formulate powers under the Defence of India Rules for the control and regulation of essential supplies. Many of these powers were delegated to the provincial governments who in turn made delegations to executive authorities, including the district officer. During 1939–42 these powers were not used in any systematic manner in the Punjab, except for gasoline rationing. A deputy commissioner might enforce restrictions for example on quantities or movements when a particular item was in short supply. It was soon evident that these off-the-cuff remedies, adopted by executives operating in small areas, were often worse than the disease, creating an artificial interference at one point with a supply system which could only be tackled effectively from source onwards. In the Punjab the subject of controls was at this stage allotted as an extra to the home secretary's department.

The bombshell came with the calamity of the Bengal famine of 1943. The rice situation in terms of price and availability deteriorated so rapidly in the winter of 1942 and the early months of 1943 that starvation and death, especially in the city of Calcutta, shook the whole country.

As the situation in Bengal developed during 1942 the central government appointed a 'Wheat Controller for India', who stopped all movement of wheat and its products from surplus provinces, including the Punjab, except on permits. This device was designed to secure information about despatches to deficit areas so that these could be utilized to feed the greatest need. This system brought negligible relief. Many permits were not honoured by the trade, if supplies or prices became difficult; at the receiving end supplies disappeared in the absence of a sound distribution agency. Some improvement was introduced by the appointment in the Punjab of 'clearing agents', selected from the wholesale trade, who became the channel for despatches. This provided certain knowledge of actual despatches. In these mounting difficulties Bombay in 1943 proceeded, on its own initiative, towards the rationing of its bigger towns. They also enforced a levy on their producers, by which the government calculated each cultivator's surplus and bought it under law at a fixed price. The Government of India now appointed the Foodgrains Policy Committee under the chairmanship of Sir Theodore Gregory, their economic adviser. I was a member of this Committee as a representative of the Punjab government. It produced in the record period of about three months a series of recommendations. These were accepted as policy and enforced under the supervision of the central government throughout the country from the winter of 1943.

The administration of food gradually but surely improved during the period 1943–47. The organization set up for purchase and distribution ensured that there could be no repetition of even the beginnings of a Bengal famine in any part of India. Imports were minimized and used to effective purpose; certainty of price and supply replaced chaotic and chancy conditions. In this process departments for food were developed and vast experience gained by the administration.

The Punjab set up in 1943 a separate department of Food and Civil Supplies. The main planks of the food administration, as these developed and were improved during the period 1943–47 on the basis of the Gregory Committee's recommendations, may now be considered.

Rationing was prescribed by the Committee as an essential for all urban areas, whether in deficit or surplus provinces, initially in all towns of 100,000 and above, to be extended progressively to towns of over 50,000, and thereafter even to smaller ones. The object of this arrangement was that all concentrations of population dependent on the farmers' surplus and on the market should be guaranteed their basic food needs in a defined ration and at a fixed price. In return they were forbidden to buy any foodgrains outside the ration, in order to guarantee that the competitive demand for supplies was reduced so significantly as to make possible procurement by the government at a reasonable price. The Punjab introduced rationing in seven towns with a population of over 100,000 and by 1947 had extended this to all towns above 50,000 and in deficit areas even to places with populations of about 20,000. The logical and practical imperative behind the rationing system was to guarantee minimum food needs in the towns, and to induce a slack in the market of such proportions as would enable government to buy at a fixed price. The Punjab went further by also providing 'controlled distribution', through fair price shops, usually on a card system, to all areas, urban or rural, which might periodically need this when supplies were short. Thus distribution arrangements meticulously catered, the whole year round, to the food needs of towns by rationing; they also had regard to those of other deficit areas, both urban and rural.

Monopoly procurement was not a specific recommendation of the Gregory Committee. At that time experience of purchasing grain was not widespread enough to permit a uniform prescription for procurement. The fact and responsibility of rationing, however, implied and indeed made unavoidable the achievement of maximum procurement. A provincial government could not merely hope to be fed by allocations from the centre. The centre was the arbiter of requirements or surpluses, in consultation with the provinces, on the basis of estimates of production and needs. Every province was thus required to lay hands on its own surplus, even though this might only be seasonal or limited to certain areas.

By 1947 the Punjab had introduced and successfully worked a monopoly procurement system for both wheat and rice, which meant that, from the point at which these foodgrains started their commercial existence, all purchase, allocation, movement, and distribution was regulated by the government. The main features of the monopoly for wheat are outlined to indicate the administrative operations undertaken:

(i) within the village wheat was permitted to be sold for local use or to a village shopkeeper, but for no other purpose;

(ii) movement from the village was permitted only to the nearest market;

(iii) at the market wheat could only be sold to the government or to an agent acting for the government, and only at the price fixed for that market;

[These provisions ensured that wheat moved outside the village came under government regulation at the first point of marketing.]

(iv) at and after the market, wheat was allotted for the various needs it had to meet. These were several:

a) for local consumption, where it was allocated to approved retailers who had to account for the supplies;

b) for despatch to rationed towns or deficit districts;

c) for storage locally (to meet demands during the leaner months);

d) for export to other provinces; and so on;

[With experience it was possible to make allocations as near as possible to the point of ultimate consumption in order to avoid extra costs of handling and cross haulage. This was important as the annual wheat surplus in the Punjab usually came into the market, to the extent of 60 to 75 per cent, immediately following harvesting at the end of April, in the months of May and June before the rains broke in July.]

(v) at each stage of handling, a predetermined tabulated set of charges were payable to the government agent, together with his margin of profit, so that the exact amounts for a variety of methods of disposal were defined and known;

(vi) these arrangements were strengthened by law which prohibited the movement of wheat from the market except by permit. An unauthorized movement was liable to check and punishment at any point of discovery.

Statutory price control was recommended as essential by the Gregory Committee, to be effected at the point of purchase, and at each subsequent stage of distribution. Any transaction at a higher price was not only a distribution offence but one under the criminal law also.

The Punjab government had stoutly opposed rationing and statutory price control before the Committee and even sent the redoubtable and fiery Choudhry Sir Chhotu Ram, who had the reputation and indeed some of the manner of 'the farmers' lion', to appear as a witness against these proposals. As a representative of the Punjab on the Committee I was required to append to its report a minute of dissent, even though discussion at its deliberations had convinced me personally that the policy recommended was necessary for the all-India food situation. Not that the Punjab case lacked reason or fact. Agricultural prices had been abysmally low for over a decade; there was small assurance that the government could effectively control the prices of the farmers' requirements, particularly cloth and kerosene, the latter used almost universally in the villages for lighting; moreover, as a heavy surplus area, with wheat-producing fields often within easy walking distance of the towns, the discipline of rationing appeared to invite an easy flouting of the law.

Centre-state relations in food were the subject of detailed controversy in the Gregory Committee. While it was agreed that distribution and rationing arrangements should be the administrative responsibility of the province, the deficit provinces urged that procurement should be the centre's responsibility to ensure adequate performance. The Gregory Committee took the view that internal procurement should be a provincial responsibility but that the overall definition of performance and requirements should be determined and supervised by the centre in a so-called annual 'basic plan' drawn up and reviewed periodically.

The practice emerged of central supervision and direction in food procurement and distribution, while executive implementation remained with the units. Central direction was, with rare exceptions, honoured. The centre also determined the administrative surcharge which a province could impose on exports. Some surplus areas near the Punjab, particularly Faridkot princely state, had seized the occasion to enhance their revenues by exports to other provinces. It was decided that two principles should limit such exactions, the first that a surcharge should be limited to administrative costs and the second that it should be payable by the local consumer also. The Punjab levied a charge of four annas per maund (equivalent to 2p for 82 lb). With its large turnover this more than covered the administrative costs of what developed into a giant organization of government.

Ancillary arrangements of considerable diversity and concentration were involved in this wholesale interference and regulation of the marketable surplus. To mention a few: (i) inspection of grain for quality, to determine whether a premium or discount on the fixed price was due, had to be both speedy and honest; (ii) storage for foodgrains had to be rented in all kinds of places and of all manner of varieties to meet the peak arrivals in the markets; (iii) at a later stage the government embarked on a programme of construction of modern grain silos with the help of a small additional surcharge; (iv) control of a rigorous kind, though not amounting to monopoly procurement, had to be introduced for the minor cereals, as their price and supply seasonally influenced the stability of the price of wheat and the willingness of the farmer to part with his surplus; the price of these grains had to be fixed and the government became a purchaser of these, particularly gram, as a cushion for the system; (v) the department became one of the biggest purchases of gunny bags used for the despatch of grain; on one occasion when gunny bag prices were rising steadily the department made a large purchase on the 'futures' market for forward delivery at a lower price; this greatly shook the auditors as highly unrespectable for a government but, as the operation saved a considerable amount of money as the price trend continued upwards, no head rolled; (vi) the development and administration of substantial anti-smuggling operations to prevent foodgrains moving across the borders, particularly to the deficit high-priced neighbour at Delhi and the hungry people of the desert of Rajasthan.

These subjects are listed as illustrative of the many-faceted organizational details involved in any systematic and large-scale interference with the flow of an essential commodity produced by thousands of farmers and required by millions of consumers. Two details require fuller treatment—the relations of the government with the trade, and the way personnel was organized.

The policy of the Punjab government was to use the food-grains trade as agents to the maximum extent possible compatible with a system of distribution and procurement controlled by the government. The trade was worked into the process on these terms. In rationed towns retailers were selected in each ward from existing shopkeepers. The consumer was at liberty to register his card with any of these and he could change his retailer if he wished, which acted as an incentive for good performance.

More complex arrangements were necessary for procurement. The extent of a man's business in a market is normally largely determined by his reaction to the prevailing price. With a fixed price, subject only to quality allowances, the bottom was knocked out of the traders' market. The existing commission agents in each market (called *pucca arhties*), who included some cooperatives, were given the first choice to form an association to act as the government's agent for purchase. They determined the extent of shareholding among themselves and registered as a legal corporate entity. The Punjab had remarkable success with these arrangements and it was only rarely that the government had to use an individual, or step in itself, to substitute for a *Pucca Arhties* Association.

Exports from the province carried bigger responsibilities. At times wagons had to be formed into a full train of fifty to sixty from several stations, and contacts maintained and running accounts kept for several receiving agencies, mostly other provincial governments. To do this work 'clearing agents', some ten in all, were selected from among wholesalers in the business. They took over the grain from the *Pucca Arhties* Association at the market or station and arranged its despatch. The commercial banks were used to clear finance, avoiding dilatory government procedures and checks, and payments were made by them to the clearing agent on the production of evidence of despatch, which was most often the railway receipt.

The government did, however, keep a reserve sanction in its own hands, by taking over a portion of the grain purchased into what was called the 'provincial reserve', including stocks for two to three months' consumption maintained under the control of each rationing controller for his town. The reserve was not of great proportions, at its maximum about 20 per cent of annual turnover, but could be used as a safeguard against untoward action by the trade and as a lever, knowledge of which helped to secure a stable price and supply level. This lever never had to be used against the trade. Possibly the very existence of the safeguard ensured that it did not need to be used.

But the Punjab was indeed fortunate in being able to operate on one of the most highly organized marketing systems in the country. In most of India villagers marketed at a weekly gathering (called the *haat*) of a few villages, at a convenient place near them. The *haat* was indeed quite an occasion for the exchange of gossip and the meeting of families, including women and children, and the families brought together all kinds of goods produced in the village, including foodgrains. The whole atmosphere was festive and social, apart from the business transacted, much of which was between villagers themselves by barter.

Most often the quantities of foodgrains brought to the *haat* were small, though the variety of goods was large.

The Punjab had never practised the weekly market. The marketing of agricultural surpluses including foodgrains, cotton, and *ghee* was done on all working days at regular, organized markets, through professional commission agents (*arhties*). These middlemen had a long tradition of dealing commercially with the ultimate buyers, who might be as far away as at Calcutta, Bombay, or Delhi. Methods were modern, including the use of correspondence, telegrams, in several places telephones, railway and truck transport, and the banking system. The *pucca arhti* represented the buyer, wherever he might be, and the *kuccha arhti* the seller, usually a farmer from the villages the market served. Each kind of *arhti* charged his clients at that time a commission of eight annas per cent on the value of the goods (equivalent to 5p on £7.50). In the 1950s this fee went up to twelve annas per cent. Sizeable quantities of foodgrains were sold all over the province in this way. The system was highly efficient considering that the commission agent had to exercise responsibility for his client not only for the quantity but for the quality of each consignment. The variations in rice were tremendous, the famed Basmati, said to originate from fields in Dehra Dun, commanding double the price of the coarse rice.

I have myself, before the monopoly system was introduced, bought large quantities of wheat on the telephone from ready arrivals in the market through commission agents. Every contract was honoured even though it was necessarily reduced to writing *post facto*. The government found this system of purchase better than by formal advertised tender, as once it became known that the government had accepted a particular price the market tended to regard it as a minimum, whereas if the government purchased from ready arrivals the price had to be determined by open bidding for that day. A system evolved later to avoid these difficulties was to buy a portion of the day's heaps in the market, in a contiguous area, after the bidding had taken place. This 'share system' had, however, to be authorized by law as the government took over grain already bid for by other buyers.

Another marked feature of the business was that it was mostly organized on a family basis and grain was often stored and looked after like an extension of the groceries and vegetables in the family kitchen. The standards of performance were therefore high, even though personal, and the schedules of cost were competitive. India had not yet generally adopted the use of chemicals for the preservation of foodgrains nor, except at ports, were there modern warehouses. These methods received, during the period of controls, a considerable fillip in various parts of the country by the government's undertaking the direct handling of foodgrains. The Punjab learnt through its provincial reserve a great deal about the storage and preservation of foodgrains, thereby considerably reducing losses by waste.

The Punjab was in these ways able to establish a regulation of food which gave the government and people the fullest use of the trade, including not only their knowledge but important facilities, such as their relations with local labour, storage, and financial and handling capacity. This successful and highly advantageous cooperation was based on two main pillars. First, there was no overlap anywhere between policy and executive responsibility as between the trade and the government. Not one grain of wheat or rice was available for disposal at the discretion of the trade; there was no mixed system. The second was that all responsibilities and the actions they required, together with the costs involved, were reduced to the most detailed instructions and wherever possible, forms. Thus, apart from the literature prepared for government executives, each operator—the retailer, the *Pucca Arhties* Association, the clearing agent, even the receiving agents of provincial governments—had a separate brochure stating exactly what he was obliged to do and the money that would be involved in each activity. The government also maintained close liaison with representatives of the trade at headquarters and, through its staff, with individuals in the markets.

Even though the trade was utilized, a large organization of officers and men had to be built up over a short period. By 1947 the Food and Civil Supplies department was one of the biggest in the government. Each rationed town was in the charge of a rationing controller, with several ward rationing officers, each dealing with a population of about 20,000. A considerable clerical staff to deal with cards and supplies to and accounts from retailers, and a small inspectorate to check cards and families, was established. Another branch of the rationing controller's staff handled the receipt, storage, and issue of foodgrains from warehouses (*godowns*) supervised by them. Procurement had a separate organization under a district food controller, who in turn had to have men at each market, and support for ancillary operations like storage, despatch, and inspection for quality. The local staffs were placed under the charge of district officers, so that the weight of the normal administration could assist them in their highly specialized operations. Headquarters not only maintained staffs for policy, law, and finance but also for several executive operations, like the planning of movement in consultation with the railways, the purchase and use of gunny bags, dealings with receiving governments, and a substantial accounts organization.

Considering the urgency and speed with which this department was established, the recruitment of personnel was inevitably mixed. Many of the top supervisory officers were taken from the permanent civil services, particularly the ICS and provincial civil service. A whole wing of the Cooperative department, headed by its registrar, I. E. Jones, who became the first director of Food Purchase in the Punjab, and his assistant, L. R. Dawar, the first chief purchase officer, was incorporated into the Food department.

The largest number of men, especially in the rank and file, were recruited by decentralized committees of officers, the more senior one under the deputy commissioner and for junior posts under the rationing controller or district food controller. There were also appropriate committees at headquarters.

In this way in a comparatively short period a large variety of men were recruited or transferred to the food organization. These were moulded into a team, eventually to a sensitive, corporate machine, by dint of detailed instruction in writing defining each man's job, by supervision, and by encouragement through promotions to those who did well. Though these men came from a variety of sources they were soon able to initiate and develop business.

As a result the government was able quite quickly to save on personnel experience and costs, by progressively handing over positions of responsibility and supervision to lower categories of trained men. This became a crucial need when in 1947 the province was partitioned and the top cadres of service lost the British altogether, and all cadres were weakened by the division of personnel. The first rationing controllers had all been men from the ICS or provincial civil service. Soon the government was able to dispense with all ICS officers in this position and most of those from the provincial civil service, and hand over the work to men who had come up the line.

The food organization established during 1943–47 was a considerable administrative achievement. The canvas it covered and regulated was large and intricate; above all there were no precedents or experience to rely on. Foodgrain surpluses come from thousands of farmers and vary from a mere maund or two which one family might sell to meet the barest necessities, to hundreds of maunds from one of the big estates in the Punjab. The number of persons who handled these surpluses in the various markets ran into thousands. The idea of accepting the responsibility for issuing a ration card to each family and every establishment in the towns, and for closing all other ways of obtaining food in a society the bulk of whose citizens were illiterate, was unheard of in India. Nonetheless the many and various operators dealing with food were knit together in a system of regulation that worked with marked efficiency. A stupendous task had been attempted and had achieved the rhythm of daily routine.

Perhaps for this very reason the standards of performance varied considerably between the provinces. While rationing was a universal practice for all sizeable towns, the system of procurement varied. At one extreme were provinces like Bombay and Madras which assessed and levied surpluses at each village. At the other extreme were those like the giant United Provinces, which never achieved high proficiency, and which shared the market between the government and the trade. In between came the Punjab with a rigorous monopoly at the first stage of commercial operations at the market. In the country as a whole, however, the standard of performance by 1947 ensured an adequate distribution of food at an assured reasonable price.

There was of course always the criticism of the existence of a black market. This was of some proportions, for example, in UP and indeed wherever the procurement system shared the grain between the government and the trade. In the Punjab a black market did exist but was of minor, negligible incidence. It was in fact in sugar rather than in foodgrains that it flourished. The reason for this was primarily social. Sugar had been rationed simultaneously with foodgrains at an equal amount for all citizens. Lower income groups, however, consumed not so much sugar as the cheaper sweetener *gur* (solidified cane juice). With an equal sugar ration for all, there was constant temptation to sell sugar to the more affluent at a profit, either directly, or in collusion with retailers.

The food system of the Punjab was put to its severest and most sudden test following the partition of the province. The East Punjab state (as it was now called) would in any case have to face food difficulties. It was the recognized official estimate that it would be deficient in both wheat and rice, as the major producing districts were in the areas (substantially) allocated to Pakistan. The East Punjab had a surplus only in gram which flourished abundantly whenever rainfall was good, particularly in the normally dry Hissar district.

But the position at partition was complicated overnight by the giant movement of populations from both sides of the border in circumstances of violence and terror. Normal life was paralysed. Transport of all kinds was either unavailable or reserved at the highest priority for the movement of refugees across the borders to safety. Food arrangements and the controlled system were able to weather this storm. As far as statistics and information can establish, not one person died of starvation in the partition avalanche. The system in its normal routine had so spread out stocks that people could be fed until the tension was relieved. It is indeed certain that in the absence of the food organizations the population would have been exposed to calamity and, with the highly inflamed emotions of the time, would have indulged in rioting and destruction. Nor is there any doubt that the use of the trade provided a resilience which purely bureaucratic arrangement would not have done. In this crisis, at a time when communications with headquarters had broken down, the system functioned with practical imagination and initiative. The trade and the bureaucracy complemented each other in a combined salvage operation. If the limitations of either threatened to thwart action, it would be effectively taken by the other.

Gradually order returned to the state, which was so able to garner its supplies and organize their distribution that by 1950 East Punjab had ceased to depend on allocated wheat from the centre to meet a part of its needs. It was even able to export small quantities of rice to other states.

With independence, however, food policy itself entered the arena of national debate at the highest level. The Congress Party, in power throughout the country, decided to reconsider policy. There was an opinion among the public that controls provided the opportunity for corruption and that it was prevalent among officials and the trade. This opinion was most strongly held in states where food controls had been least effectively enforced. These included UP, Bihar, and Madhya Pradesh; of these the first two enjoyed considerable political influence. Deficit states, especially Madras and Bombay, were apprehensive about controls being removed. East Punjab shared the view that it was premature to do so. India was still importing food; conditions were by no means stabilized and the basis for decontrol was problematic and shaky.

The central government's attitude was cautious yet questioning. The strongly held views of Mahatma Gandhi against controls, however, decisively tilted the balance. The decontrol of food was decided on at a conference of food ministers in the late autumn of 1947, where Gandhi himself addressed the ministers and their officials. He explained in a post-prayer address later on 8 December 1947:

The object of the removal [of controls] is not to lower the prices at a bound, it is to return to normal life. Superimposed control is bad any day. And it is worse in this country, in that we are a nation of millions, spread over a large area . . . When the control is removed the nation will breathe free, it will have the right to make mistakes and correcting them in the proper way . . . Any government worth the name has to show the nation how to face deficits, bad weather and other handicaps of life, through its collective effort, instead of its being effortlessly helped to live anyhow. Thus considered decontrol means that the business of foresight is transferred from the few members of the government to the millions composing the nation.

The Mahatma did not live to see the results of decontrol, removed as he was at the hands of his assassin on 30 January 1948. The price and supply position reacted adversely within days. The food ministers, meeting in the autumn of 1948, resolved that within a year, and more quickly where possible, the country should move back to the 'status quo ante', to a system of control in each state as rigorous as it used to be.

The Punjab went back by April 1949 to the same system it had proceeded to dismantle the previous year. But in this process of switch off and switch on, the country as a whole lost crucially in clarity of objectives and action, and above all in morale. In many states vital concessions and compromises were made which obscured and damaged the principles of a real control system. That system was not restored but replaced by an inadequate patchwork.

Much of the argument about controls had assumed corruption, and the whole food administration effort became tainted and smeared in the public mind. Yet if this suspicion had been more fully analysed it would have been noticed that complaint about corruption was loudest in states where inadequate control had functioned. Where full controls covering the whole supply line systematically had been administered, there was little dissatisfaction, and that usually directed only at details.

The Government of India soon realized that the country was indeed getting the worst of both worlds. Policy accepted the responsibilities of control in feeding the people; performance was compromised by lack of will and consequent concessions. Meanwhile imports, and the foreign exchange for them, were a running drain on money needed for development. Following a food ministers' meeting the government in February 1950 appointed the Foodgrains Procurement Committee. The chairman was Thirumala Rao, MP, and in addition to him there were three civil service experts, of whom I was one. The report of this Committee, delivered in June 1950, completed my official association with the administration of food.

The Thirumala Rao Committee examined the practical experience of all the states since the Gregory Committee's report of 1943. It made detailed proposals for each but in principle its main recommendations were:

(i) distribution, which means effective rationing in all urban areas at least, was the base and key to the food problem. Only a fully operative rationing system could produce the stable conditions necessary to achieve procurement at a reasonable price.

(ii) sufficient experience had now been gained to recommend a uniform system of procurement throughout India (except for those states which had an effective levy at the village level, who should continue with this). This system was one in which monopoly procurement is established at the first point where foodgrains entered their commercial life. In the description of such a system the report used the Punjab model.

These recommendations were stillborn, as the report was not even formally considered by the governments of the states and the Union. This result was again at least partly due to a powerful personality, that of Rafi Ahmad Kidwai, a minister of cabinet rank in the Union and later appointed, in May 1952, as food minister, which portfolio he continued to hold until his death in October 1954. Kidwai, who came from UP, was an adamant decontroller. Moreover he was also a strong and influential politician, with great charm of manner, a most extensive and varied set of contacts and public relations, and a skilled operator.

Food policy ambled along, no new definition or emphasis following from the Thirumala Rao Committee's report. Further compromises with the controlled system continued to be made variously in the states. Some converted rationing to the maintenance of fair price shops where foodgrains from the government were made available seasonally when there was a shortage, but the consumer could also buy for himself when able. In some states deals were made with the trade that a percentage of purchases should be handed over to the government at a fixed price while the balance could seek their own price in the market. In most states political bosses began to make appointments of retailers and the like on the basis of patronage, ignoring previous experience or capacity. There were a number of variations in expedients, but the net result was a disintegration and evasion of the controlled system.

East Punjab stuck to its regulatory arrangements as firmly as before, but in 1951, on central direction, it surrendered over the decontrol of gram. The crop that year was poor and there was some shortage at Delhi where the *tongawallas* (horse cart owners) headed an agitation and claimed their animals were not getting their feed. The central government insisted that Punjab should remove its restrictions on movement and in effect its price and supply control. Apart from East Punjab, there were other states also which continued a highly regulated system of distribution and procurement. These included Bombay, Madras, Mysore, and the surplus state of Orissa.

Gradually, but surely, Kidwai got his way and controls were eventually formally abandoned in 1954. Freedom of price and movement was prescribed throughout the country. Individual states continued to buy quantities of foodgrains in the market as a safeguard for lean months and also for marginal distribution when necessary. Bombay even went on with the rationing of its bigger towns. The Union government continued to import foodgrains to build 'buffer stocks' and meet urgent needs. By the time of Kidwai's death at the end of 1954, decontrol in this manner had become the order of the land.

The dramatic return of the food problem in 1973-74 lies outside the scope of this narrative. However, it has important administrative aspects and implications and is for that reason discussed at Appendix I.

4

THE EAST PUNJAB—NEW-BORN FROM
THE BLOODBATH, 1947–1956

The transfer of power from the British to the Indian government was, in its last stages, highly cooperative. Of this the appointment of Viceroy Mountbatten as India's first Governor-General was the symbol. The Governor-General was now merely constitutional head of the country and Mountbatten himself was most concerned that he should give not the slightest impression of wielding power. It was however more than symbolic, because in the overwhelming problems that beset the nation Mountbatten was accepted and trusted as guide, counsellor, and friend. He exercised crucial influence as well as displaying a warm friendship. His experience, goodwill, and above all excellent public relations were used in meeting the difficulties resulting from partition, the uncertainties surrounding the princely states, and the first military encounter with Pakistan in October 1947.

In the central government, and in the states, the Indian National Congress was in dominating command. Mahatma Gandhi had used his influence to ensure that Nehru would be selected as Prime Minister without friction, and that the powerful party leader Sardar Vallabhbhai Patel would join forces with him, 'like two oxen' at the plough. This partnership was a fine amalgam of aspiration and reality that put India on the rails of stability and sound governance. Here again Mountbatten's contribution was significant for he knew, respected, and had influence with both Nehru and Patel, and often smoothed the way for their mutual comprehension and corporate effort.

For the Punjab, however, the main fact in August 1947 was not independence but partition. It was immediately plunged into bloodshed and terror and crowded out with refugees. There was a clean sweep of the minority communities, Hindus and Sikhs on one side and Muslims on the other, between both Punjabs (Indian and Pakistani) at the point of the sword. Even before 15 August, the date for the transfer of power, thousands of refugees were on the roads seeking safety in one or the other part of the to-be-divided Punjab; at and after independence numbers swelled to hundreds of thousands, and in days to millions. East Punjab eventually absorbed 2,468,000, while the neighbouring princely state—later called PEPSU (Patiala and East Punjab States Union) and merged in 1956 with the Punjab—received a further

380,000. These figures however do not sufficiently indicate the extent of the movement and dislocation. It is estimated that five million people from West Pakistan, and a similar number from East Punjab and the rest of north India crossed the frontiers, most of them through the land border of the partitioned Punjab, which was the gateway to safety by both rail and road.

The 'relief and rehabilitation' problem that this calamity created had significant influence on the political, administrative, and human situation in the new state for at least a decade. This account is not concerned with either the rights and wrongs of responsibility for the orgy of violence that caused the problem, or with the measures taken to meet and mend it. But administrative features stand out.

The credentials of the land revenue system were put to a severe and unforeseen test, and stood up to it with distinction. Most of the 'displaced persons', as official terminology described the refugees, had to be settled on land left behind by those who went to Pakistan. A cut in ownership, with proportionately larger reductions for bigger owners, was applied as India had 2.4 million 'standard acres' to distribute against 3.9 million left behind in Pakistan. The 'standard acre' itself was a concept evolved during rehabilitation to assess the value of land, with reference to its productivity, so as to ensure an equitable distribution between the claimants in terms of the value of the land due to each. Thus two acres of unirrigable land might well be equal to one acre of irrigated. Displaced persons were allotted land on the basis of their rights as ascertained from the revenue records; this also applied to other persons dependent on land, such as tenants and workers attached to particular villages in Pakistan. The accuracy of the record as an arbiter of claims was an essential instrument of rehabilitation, for land is a matter which people in the Punjab will not forget and on which they will not surrender if there is any suspicion of substantial injustice. Several thousands of families were resettled in this way with overall satisfaction, a tribute to the veracity of the land recording system.

Tribute is also due to the administration, which performed a most difficult task, involving massive detailed work; plans and operations had to be coordinated between all the departments of government in order immediately to find shelter and necessities for the displaced and then to frame the programme for resettling them. Food was one aspect and has been considered in Chapter 3. The manner in which the whole problem was met and the speed and success with which it was disposed of suggests that the Punjab administration, in spite of the lacunae created by the loss of British personnel and the disruption from the division of all the services, was a highly efficient organization. The displaced persons were resettled with energy and generally acknowledged equity as well as with constructive effect. A somewhat similar operation in Bengal lingered on and became a running sore, the scars of which are not obliterated even today. While most of the administrative work was done by the state government, it was fully backed, particularly in respect of most of the cost, by the centre which accepted relief and re-habilitation as a national responsibility.

Greater credit, and the biggest praise, must be given to the tenacity, hard work, consistent optimism, and versatility of the refugees them-selves. Those who had no land to fall back on spread all over India to re-establish themselves; many with land had to find supplementary occupations; those who remained on their new farms had to learn how to exploit and improve them. These millions of people did not produce any beggars. They rose to the challenge and provided 'the response' of success. Most of these families in fact did better for themselves, with the bigger opportunities that independence provided, than they had done in their original homes in Pakistan, and often better also than their compatriots in India. Delhi particularly was overrun by Punjabis and owes much of its present vitality to the infusion of these hard-working, albeit aggressive and often domineering, people. Partition produced the need to seize opportunities to provide work and experience for women. A lower middle class family, turned out of Pakistan overnight, now found that the qualifications which the daughters of the house had acquired for the marriage market were an immediate asset to help earn the family's food, by teaching, working in a refugee camp, or getting whatever employment was available. Today work for women is an accepted practice among these people. Partition cleared many decks for greater emancipation.

At partition the East Punjab—also called 'Punjab India' and later and finally, when Pakistan gave up using the word Punjab in its change to West Pakistan, again simply Punjab—comprised the bulk of thirteen of the twenty-nine districts of the old province, with a population of 12.4 of its former 28.4 millions. It was however distinctly the poor relation. The bulk of the irrigation system was in Pakistan's Punjab; there was not one 'canal colony' district in the East. Agriculturally a great deal of the East, particularly Hissar, parts of Rohtak, and the Karnal and Ambala districts, were prone to drought and even famine. The university and higher school educational systems had been con-centrated and had flourished in Lahore. By administrative, official, and economic standards East Punjab did not assure security or inspire optimism.

In this depressing picture there were two bright spots. The city of Amritsar, with the Golden Temple of the Sikhs, was the focus of veneration for one of India's great religions. It was also one of the biggest wholesale markets in the north, famed especially for clothing, its variety in saris attracting trousseau-seekers even from Delhi. Simla was 'the queen of hill stations', 6,000 feet up in the Himalayas, its sequestered shady walks a veritable pedestrian's paradise, its atmosphere a reminder of the summer capital of the *Raj*. It was part of the lore of Kipling's Anglo-India, and you could still almost hear his *bandar* (monkey) saying:

> No, never in my life
> Have I flirted at Faletti's
> With another *bandar*'s wife.

It was indeed difficult to think of the original Simla, used as a penal settlement during Sikh rule, when criminals sentenced to life transportation were taken up to Dagshai on the way to Simla and left there to eke out an existence in the hills beyond. In fact *Dag* (mark) *Shahi* (of the king or regime) referred to their branding at what became, and still remains, a charming military station in the hills.

In spite of Simla, however, the new state had no capital large enough to hold its government. Simla had been used as an officers' summer headquarters by both the central and the Punjab governments in the British period. The 'men' and many of the junior officers remained in the plains and the *dak* (official mail, including big files) went up and down daily from Lahore and Delhi. The East Punjab government now reversed this procedure. The Secretariat with the men were at Simla, the Governor and ministers at Jullandar, more accessible to all parts of the state to deal with the immediate crisis following partition. Offices were, however, scattered all over the state wherever accommodation could be found. As normality returned, Simla did become the effective state capital for the core of the departments and the secretariat. It was not, however, until 1953, with the completion of the first phase of the building of Chandigarh, that the whole headquarters of government could start to come together in a single location.

Politically East Punjab was a responsible democracy on 15 August 1947, the date of partition. Power was vested in the cabinet answerable to the state legislature. The latter, pending the adoption of a constitution for the country, comprised some eighty-one members of the Legislative Assembly (MLAs) inherited by this part of the divided province, including those who had left Pakistan even though their constituencies continued there. Most members of the Zamindara Party now stepped into Congress; this was neither surprising nor a matter for criticism, for the provincial party had been basically in sympathy with the cause of independence. The Muslim members of the party, left in Pakistan, were politically decimated, for their very gestures of preserving unity among the religions were now looked back upon as disloyalty to the whole idea of Pakistan, based on the principle of religion determining nationality. Their able leader, Khizar Hayat Khan, was permanently ousted from politics and made no attempt to compromise.

In the East Punjab cabinet Congress dominated. The first chief minister was Dr Gopi Chand Bhargava, an old Congressman of Hissar district elected from the University constituency. He and Swaran Singh formed the ministry till late September 1947 when it was expanded to include a team of seven in all. In this cabinet Sardar Partap Singh Kairon of Amritsar district was also included.

There were strong and determined rivalries for power within the party, and during the nine years to 1956 no undisputed political boss emerged who could hold it together. Ministers changed frequently, though at that time the cabinet remained small. (The habit of large ministries, placating the ambitions of several groups and several men, had not yet developed.) The Food and Civil Supplies department, for example, had from August 1947 to the end of December 1950 as many as six different ministers, one of them for as short a period as a week.

Two main contestants competed for leadership and alternately one or the other was chief minister, constantly looking over his shoulder to maintain a majority in the party and often displaced in the process. Dr Gopi Chand Bhargava was by temperament and character slow to act, unruffled, patient. He left much of the initiative to the administration or to more zealous colleagues. He was a quiet and salutary influence in a situation where opinion was often angry and clamorous from the aftermath of partition. He had a calm, soothing presence, could listen long and work hard. No major vices or great aspirations were attributed to him. He acquired a reputation for depending on astrologers, but the subjects on which he took their advice appeared harmless, such as the most auspicious day to open a college, or to start a tour, a subject of amusement rather than suspicion.

His rival for leadership was Bhim Sen Sachar, also a Congressman of some years' standing who had been finance minister for a short time in the Unionist pre-independence coalition government. He had done considerable work in municipal organizations, had organized an insurance company, and was a competent businessman. Sachar was energetic, conscious of his importance, could only be met by appointment, and was keen on definition, protocol, and propriety. Sachar had drive and ideas and a high reputation for integrity. He never, however, got fully into the saddle.

Until the general election of 1952, Gopi Chand remained chief minister, except for six months in 1949 when Sachar replaced him, and nine months prior to the election during which President's rule took over the administration.

During the six months when Sachar was chief minister he changed the chief secretary, appointing B. R. Tandon to replace M. R. Sachdev. There was a furore, as the latter contended that he should be allowed to complete a tenure of four to five years and implied that his transfer was inspired by prejudice. Tandon merely reacted, 'You see the trouble there is when gentlemen of the judiciary take executive positions.' This referred to the fact that both Sachdev and the home secretary, Nawab Singh, had been transferred near independence from the judicial service to the secretariat. All three officers were of the ICS. The Governor, Trivedi, seemed to consider there was some justice in Sachdev's view and informally even the central government was asked to use its good offices as protector of the services. The appointment was in the final event reversed. Sachdev returned as chief secretary, the timing corresponding with Sachar's quitting the chief minister's position. This incident suggests that 'the system' was at this time strong, particularly as the idea of tenure was a matter of convention rather than of rule or law. The position was also in marked contrast with developments during the next two decades when chief secretaries in the Punjab were discarded with as little ceremony as the skin of a banana. Another feature of Sachar's short tenure was that Gopi Chand Bhargava continued in his cabinet as finance minister. The fight was well within 'the family' of the all-embracing Congress.

Gopi Chand came back to the chief minister's position but in mid-1951 Governor Trivedi reported to the Union government that the rivalries in the Congress Party had gone so far that a period of President's rule, preceding the election of 1952, was desirable to maintain good administration. The Punjab thus achieved the unenviable distinction of being the first state in India to use these emergency powers of the constitution. For this period, June 1951 to April 1952, Trivedi was in effect the cabinet, responsible through central ministers to the Union Parliament. The state budget presented in February 1952, for example, was passed by Parliament on the initiative of the Union finance minister.

The new Indian constitution was effective law from 26 January 1950 and under it the first general election, based on universal suffrage, took place in 1952, returning 126 MLAs to the Punjab Assembly. Bhim Sen Sachar commanded a majority in the Congress legislative party and became chief minister. Gopi Chand tenaciously continued for the rest of his career to hold governmental positions of one sort or another, ending as chairman of the Khadi and Village Industry Board, a post which he held till his death in December 1966.

Alas for Sachar, however, for during his period Partap Singh Kairon had worked himself into a position of mass popularity with the new and bigger electorate. As a member of Sachar's cabinet his opinion had to be respected and even deferred to where he felt strongly. There could hardly have been a greater contrast in personality and values than between these two men. Kairon was a Jat with the manner and style, the immense energy, and many of the prejudices of the farmer. He was restive with procedures, rules, and even the law. He spoke with fury against slow precedent-directed action and said he would lead the Punjab with speed towards agricultural development and industrialization. Kairon was a furious and untidy man, always in colossal haste. Sachar's position as chief minister was thus increasingly uncomfortable, and in January 1956 he was ousted by internal manipulations within the party. Partap Singh Kairon became chief minister. In the general election of 1957 he was able to obtain a decisive verdict not only for Congress but also for many of his own nominees as MLAs. The Punjab had after almost ten years of confusion produced a political chief with the urge and capacity for unrivalled power.

Yet there was during this period a remarkable continuity of policy and of concentrated administrative effort, which worked unimpeded in spite of the strife and manoeuvres within the Congress Party. Evidence of this is the fact that the Punjab in record time pulled itself out of the agony and chaos of partition and enabled millions of displaced persons to settle down with self-reliance, and indeed to make a positive contribution to the community. The administration showed no cracks during this test, rather, indeed, resilience, imagination, and the capacity to both mend and build.

Part of this situation was the undoubted and manifest belief of members of the services that the independence of India was a matter of pride, a great opportunity. They shared with the people of the Punjab the will for effort and the determination to succeed.

The character, history, and quality of the central leadership had a strong and universal impact. Both bureaucracy and people accepted and admired the outstanding contribution to Indian self-respect and freedom of Gandhi, Jawaharlal Nehru, and Patel, to mention only three of the remarkable group of men and women who influenced or were in the government. There was an almost reflex will and discipline to serve this leadership. This was specially so in the Punjab, where it was recognized that the division of the country had created responsibilities requiring the effort and resources of the whole nation.

Sardar Patel was the dominating influence with the services. As home minister he stood out again and again for the value of independent advice from officials and the need for continuity of administration. Even though the bulk of the services, particularly the ICS and the state civil service, had been inherited from and thus 'smeared' by association with British masters, Patel made it clear that he would extend to them, by precept and deed, his fullest support. He died in December 1950 but he set a pattern that determined the initial relationship between political masters and the civil service, enabling a constructive functional contribution by each.

It would, however, be incorrect to assume that the Union government constantly interfered in the administrative business of the Punjab. The centre was at that time meticulous, even hair-splitting, in its insistence that the division of responsibilities as between centre and states should be carefully observed in practice as well as in the procedures and the process of law. Yet, by its qualitative presence, it influenced the attitudes and actions of both political masters and the services in the state. There were occasions when its influence was also used, not in direction or control, but in adjustments between the men in power in the state.

Nor would it be correct to conclude that the ministers in the state kept on the sidelines of the administrative arena. With the zest of new power, most of them took an eager interest in their subjects, and were in constant touch with their departments and the people. All of them practised a tradition held in high esteem in the folklore about Indian rulers, that of being available and accessible to the public. They were constantly, even too constantly, on tour and were the recipients of endless complaints from all manner of men.

From the first day of independence the administration was indeed in politics; politics influenced the administration and administrators learnt to be sensitive to politics. This was not surprising. Most of the men concerned, both political leaders and civil servants, had taken part in or watched the struggle for freedom, carried on within the terms and ideals of British concepts of self-government. They had longed for, and indeed breathed, the air of a democratic political system even before it was fully achieved. They fell to their parts in it as if these had been rehearsed. That the politician at the time did not interfere with day-to-day administration generally, but kept broadly to policy and public relations, was because he chose to do so, as part of his view of the political role, not because he was kept out by the 'steel frame' of colonial rule and habit.

No account of administration in the East Punjab would be complete without mention of its first Governor, Sir Chandu Lal M. Trivedi. He had been knighted by the British but was called Mister after 1947. He had been a British regime governor in Orissa, and the first and only Indian ever appointed to the position of defence secretary. 'When I was in Orissa . . .' was a favourite starting gambit of his, when giving advice to the Punjab ministers, until Swaran Singh, the home minister of East Punjab, reminded him that it was the tradition in the north that when a man married a second time he desisted from constant reference to his first wife. Trivedi forgot Orissa.

Trivedi was ostensibly a constitutional Governor; actually he wielded tremendous power, although he took pains to cloak it in the forms of influence. He operated through sub-committees of the cabinet which the chief minister was persuaded to set up on all subjects of importance, as for example 'Grow More Food', 'Relief and Rehabilitation' and 'Anti-Corruption'. Here the relevant ministers and their officers met, with Trivedi in the chair, and went through much of the more important business of government, in advance of, and often in preparation for, cabinet meetings, to which policy and important matters were referred, and at which the chief minister presided and the Governor was not present. Trivedi nourished and maintained his influence by the accumulation of detailed knowledge through written notes and discussions with officials. He established contacts with the relevant ministers and officers of the central government. He was meticulous in invariably keeping the minister concerned in the Punjab in touch, often by letter, with what he was doing. He was often able to anticipate events and prepare the ground for directed solutions.

He was the main coordinator and supervisor of policy and crucial administration while Gopi Chand Bhargava was in office. Sachar was somewhat restive about his methods and influence, but the Governor had attained such deep knowledge of the problems of the state that Sachar was not able to resist his guidance. Trivedi remained an effective and operating force until he left the Punjab in March 1953. He played a vital, indeed monumental, role in its administration. No subsequent Governor exercised any comparable influence.

The Punjab cabinet was responsible to the lower house, the *Vidhan Sabha* (the legislative assembly with MLAs) but the state had also opted under the relevant constitutional provision for an upper house, the *Vidhan Parishad* (the legislative council with MLCs). The latter were mostly elected from specialized interests, a few were nominated by the Governor on the advice of his cabinet. One-third retired every two years after a six-year tenure.

The powers and rights of members were defined by parliamentary procedure based on British practice and expressed primarily through debate, legislation, questions, committees, and the budget. Although much time, and a great deal of paper and printing, were devoted to the required procedures, the MLA and MLC, particularly the former, wielded more influence outside than in the house. The members' relations to political power were expressed through party groupings and focused chiefly on leadership contests and patronage. In a situation of delicately balanced factions the potential sanction of withdrawal of support from the chief minister and ministers was important and the MLA became an influence to reckon with. He was able to exert pressure on the local administration, mostly to obtain concessions for himself and his men on matters such as licences, local jobs, and positions of prestige or power. Generally during this period the MLA was by no means a crucial or overriding influence. However, his presence was registered in the minds of officials; he was seen as a person who had to be treated with the greatest attention, an unavoidable, though not over-powering, nuisance and busybody. In the legislature he was afforded all the information he sought but on the whole treated rather superficially and his vote taken for granted. The Punjab produced no great standard of debate in the house, and speeches were generally regarded as froth and bubble rather than reasoned statements weighing the pros and cons of policy or law. They seldom had the distinction of knowledge or brilliance; they did have sparkles of humour and occasional elo-quence.

There was also at the time broad agreement about the objectives of policy. The relief and rehabilitation problem was regarded as a high priority. In other matters so much that was basic and minimal had to be done everywhere—schools, dispensaries, main roads, irrigation, and electricity—that resources, rather than choices or refinements, were the determining factor.

The only point on which opinion was strongly divided was the major regional issue of 'Punjabi Suba'. This was the question whether the Punjabi-speaking part of the state, generally to the west and adjoin-ing Pakistan and Jammu, should become a separate entity from the Hindi-speaking area to the south and east. The matter was not, how-ever, as simple as that as these two areas were also the dividing line between the Sikh-majority and Hindu-majority portions of the state. It became a bitter bone of contention between the two communities. In the state as it stood Hindus predominated with a population of 8.12 mil-lion as against 3.83 million Sikhs (1951 census). If the state was divided the Sikhs would have a small majority in the Punjabi region.

The Sikhs felt they had suffered the greatest blow from partition. They had left an affluent area for a poorer one; they distinguished their position from that of the Hindus who left Pakistan, on the ground that the latter had joined the overwhelming majority of their co-religionists in India. While almost all Sikh sentiment subscribed to this general view, on the specific issue of Punjabi Suba opinion among them was strongly divided between the political following of Congress and that of the Akali Party. The Akalis made Suba their platform; Congress had thus far not decided in favour of it, and indeed during this period was opposed to a further division of this frontier state.

The Hindus of the region bitterly opposed Punjabi Suba. They feared it as a means whereby the Sikhs would impose their culture and religion on them. Many went so far as to declare their mother tongue falsely as Hindi, not Punjabi, in the 1951 census, in an endeavour to keep the statistics in their favour. The census became the occasion of serious tension in some towns; special provision had to be made to maintain law and order. The Hindus organized a body known as the

Hindi Raksha Samiti to combat the Sikh demand for a Punjabi-speaking state.

The struggle was complicated by the question of scripts. The Sikh scripture was written in *Gurmukhi*, which is a distinctive variant of the *Devanagiri* script used for Hindi. The Akalis pressed for the use not only of Punjabi but of the *Gurmukhi* script also. Hindus opposed this vehemently, particularly angered that their children should have to acquire an additional script at school.

Many of the extreme fears and suspicions expressed by both sides were without basis in fact. Historically and culturally the two religions and communities were inextricably and happily connected. The Sikhs had been regarded as the saviours of Hindu culture from Muslim persecution. There was a strong tradition in the Punjab for Hindu families to offer one of their sons, often the eldest, to the *Khalsa* (the Sikh congregation) as a soldier to protect their religion. Inter-marriage between Hindus and Sikhs was widespread. In many Hindu families a room would be set apart in the house to locate the *Granth Sahib* (the Sikh Bible). The Sikh form of worship, particularly the ritual of hymn-singing and the practice of the congregation being also a social entity, attracted many Hindus, who had always had free access to the *gurdawaras* (Sikh temples). On the other hand the Sikhs were by no means a backward community compared with the Hindus. They not only held their own, but indeed dominated almost every branch of life in East Punjab. They had also made their way in successful competition in all parts of India. About half their population (total Sikhs, 1951 census, 6.2 million) lived outside the Punjab.

Nevertheless, feelings ran high over *Punjabi Suba* and these became polarized in terms of Hindu versus Sikh. Politically, however, *Suba* was not widely considered a practical proposition. Congress, which had not yet opted for it, included in its following the majority of Sikhs in the Punjab. A minister like Partap Singh Kairon, himself a Sikh, developed into the most bitter opponent of the demand. Thus the idea and politics of *Punjabi Suba* did not at this stage have any marked influence on administrative policy. There was nonetheless an acute awareness, all through the government, of the Sikh presence as a factor to be considered in administrative decisions involving any kind of patronage, including employment. This was reflected, for example, in selecting personnel for the services and for various positions in government, from the choice of ministers down to the appointment of peons. The Sikhs thus fully enjoyed the importance and benefits that a powerful minority will inevitably secure in a democracy.

The *Punjabi Suba* cry provoked opposition and also the growth of other inherent regional pressures. People in the hills began to think about a separate unit for themselves. Their economic priorities differed of necessity from those of the plains. They generally understood Hindi, and many of them Punjabi, but their own spoken languages were dialects from the main linguistic sources of the north, and were grouped together under the composite name *Pahari* (literally meaning the language of the hills). Himachal Pradesh, comprising many small princely areas, including a few sizeable chunks of territory, had already been established as a Union Territory under a chief commissioner in 1948; its later elevation to become a state owed something to the pressures from the hill peoples.

The spread and strengthening of the idea that the Hindi region of the state should be formed into Haryana owed much to the Jat tradition which was dominant there. The Jats were numerically a minority but the single largest and most self-conscious group; with perhaps less than complete historical accuracy they associated their heritage with the Kavravas and Pandavas, who had fought, centuries before Christ, the battles of the Mahabharata, and produced the inimitable Bhagavad Gita, 'the song celestial', on and around the battlefields of Kurukshetra. Haryana in this way boasted descent from the foundations of Hindu civilization. These feelings, 'clouds no bitter than a man's hand', grew and eventually produced a further division of the Punjab State to make reality conform to urges, dreams, and aspirations.

The considered view of the government on the whole question of states was embodied in the States Reorganization Act which came into force on 1 November 1956. It was based on the report of a commission which made extensive enquiries and submitted comprehensive recommendations. The Act, far from conceding *Punjabi Suba*, provided that the Punjab should include within it the state known as PEPSU, which had been formed in 1948. Thus Punjab added six districts to its thirteen, and a population of 3.5 millions to its 12.6 (1951 census). This additional population was almost exactly 50 per cent Sikh (1.7 million).

It was obvious that the desire of the nation was for a bigger and stronger frontier state. It was hoped that time and usage would unite it. One concession to meet the situation was provision for what came to be called the 'regional formula', which set up two regional committees, comprising members of the legislature from the Punjabi and Hindi areas, and introduced procedures to incorporate these committees' views in the development programmes of the state. This formula never took on any positive life and did not become an active element in either policy formulation or administration in the Punjab.

The heat generated by the *Punjabi Suba* problem influenced the action taken on two practical matters, namely the language to be used in the administration and in schools.

In the administration it was obvious that a change could not be made overnight. A whole generation of civil servants would have to attain proficiency in the use of another language. Urdu had been the official language used at and below the district level. All the officials were acquainted with it, as were also the literate public and their intermediaries such as lawyers. Forms and registers were in Urdu. To start with, therefore, the government prescribed that all officials must pass departmental tests in the regional languages, Hindi and Punjabi. Most of them did so and promptly forgot their written use through lack of practice. Meanwhile Urdu continued to be used.

Some of the work at district level, and most of it at the division and at government headquarters, was done in English. The argument about the competing rights of Punjabi (in the *Gurmukhi* script) and Hindi (in the *Devanagiri* script) tended to prolong the *status quo* in favour of English. It was indeed only after the further division of the Punjab in 1966 that any really serious attempt was made to substitute local languages for English at the headquarters of government.

In education, however, a decision could not be postponed. Hindi had been declared the future official language of the union and it was therefore generally agreed that it must be taught in schools from the middle levels onwards. Because English was important as an international language and was the key to scientific knowledge, it was also agreed that it should be used, or at least be available as a subject, especially at the higher school and university levels. The dispute therefore related to the medium of instruction at the primary stage. Should it be Hindi or Punjabi, or a variation of both? The language also inevitably involved the script. In 1949 the 'Sachar formula' was evolved to meet the rival claims. It provided that the regional language, the mother tongue, should be the medium of instruction in each of the two regions. But it specified that if a defined number of children (or their parents) in a particular school desired teaching through the other language, this should be provided. This formula assuaged feelings and was accepted. It assumed that adequate teaching facilities could be made available in both languages. This was, in smaller and more remote places, a hope rather than a fact, but it was never considered an impediment of any importance. The schools muddled through.

These early experiments with the change of languages produced some interesting situations. Most of the adult generation knew Urdu, and were now faced with the predicament of their children coming to them of an evening with homework in Hindi or Punjabi. Urdu also lingered on in practice and sentiment. At the height of tension, on the *Punjabi Suba* issue, Pandit Nehru remarked in a public address at Chandigarh, that while people argued at length about Hindi or Punjabi, they seemed to do so mostly in Urdu.

Fortunately the ordinary variety of Hindi, or Hindusthani, as spoken, has much in common with Urdu, and persons speaking either language can ordinarily understand each other. Even Punjabi can be largely followed by them. The scripts, however, differ radically between Hindi, written from left to right and Urdu based on the Arabic tradition. In fact one of the fears in the Punjab and the north was that the south, which was in the early years not opposed to Hindi, would learn it from scratch in the more Sanskritized vocabulary and then steal a march on the north as they had earlier done in English. This fear of more classical Hindi continues. In a recent convocation address the late Balraj Sahn, a Punjabi and a much idolized actor, said that All-India Radio instead of announcing, 'You will now hear the news in Hindi,' should, in view of the abstruse Hindi they used, for accuracy's sake say 'You will now hear Hindi in the news.'

English, while given less importance by precept, grew in real significance because of its practical value in modern life. This situation produced an inverted snobbery. While the best educated, particularly some of the top politicians, were anxious on social and public occasions to show off their facility in the local language in preference to English, the plumber, mason, electrician, and car mechanic would go out of his way to show off his limited English vocabulary, using as many words as he could, whenever he could. With the departure of the British, the quality of both spoken and written English deteriorated. Its quantity on the other hand increased. This trend toward English is now reinforced by the adamant opposition of the south to the use of Hindi as the exclusive national official language. English shows every sign of remaining and spreading rather than diminishing in India. A factor which has given this development a further fillip is the desire of the outside world to read more about India by Indians. There is now a bigger audience for Indians in the English-speaking world than when India was a British imperial possession.

The beginnings of significant changes in the public service were also apparent in these years. By 1956 most of the senior middle positions in the state government were held by officers of the Indian Administrative Service. The ICS filled only a few of the top positions in the state, many ICS men having gone to the centre to meet the expansion of the ministries there. The Punjab again scored a first, in the appointment in 1956 of a woman, Sarla Khanna of the IAS, as a collector. There had also been an expansion of the services. Whole areas of new activity, such as community development, had been opened up by the government. This rapid expansion, which continued for several years following independence, produced a series of fresh problems with reference to competence, training, adequate job definitions, and homogeneity of teams of workers.

By 1950 the Punjab had selected the site at Chandigarh for its new capital. This was no doubt chosen partly on account of regional pressures, as it lies almost exactly on the dividing line between the Punjabi and Hindi regions and was therefore acceptable to both. The selectors had, however, not reckoned with history, as this location provided a bitter bone of contention when the regions became two separate states in 1966, and both Punjab and Haryana claimed it. Chandigarh as a capital was an otherwise admirable choice, commanding easy access from all parts of the state, and placed at the foothills of the Himalayas in command of vistas most pleasing to the eye.

In human and social relations a new dimension was added to administrative life. The elected representatives of the people, whether ministers or political leaders, were now the senior and directing partners of the bureaucratic elite in the conduct of government, the former clothed in the mantle and majesty of the chosen, the latter an unavoidable necessity. A relationship of tolerance and even good humour developed, though there were sharp and manifest differences in ways of life and dress. The politicians invariably dressed Indian style, mostly in the Congress tradition, using handspun cloth (khadi), the bureaucrats almost invariably in European style. The politician never served alcohol and could not afford to be seen with a drink in public; the bureaucracy did not practise abstinence. These distinctions tended to weaken over the years. The bush shirt and the dying away of the khadi tradition assisted the process. Certain core differences still remain though other possibly more subtle characteristics mark the cleavage.

By 1956 East Punjab had in many ways come through the main pangs of creation. The rehabilitation of displaced persons had been accomplished; the state had elected its rulers in 1952 on a basis of universal suffrage; it had substantially built a new capital at Chandigarh, where its government started functioning from 1953; it had absorbed PEPSU into its jurisdiction; it had expanded its services and programmes. It was prepared for deeper change, some kind of 'take-off'.

It was against this background that Partap Singh Kairon stepped in as the undisputed political leader of the Punjab and its chief minister. Real and formal power were combined in his person.

5

FINANCE FOR DEVELOPMENT, 1950–1953

The Finance department of the Punjab, working under the administrative supervision of the finance secretary and the policy direction of the finance minister, spent much of its time and energy in the scrutiny of demands for expenditure from the several departments of the government. These would include approval of the personnel requirements of projects including remuneration and allowances; the sanction of estimates for all the bigger 'works'; the examination of foreign exchange needs, claims for which had to receive the approval of the central government; and a variety of cases, trivial and significant, in which a variation from precedent was in any way involved.

The main responsibility of the Finance department was, however, to prepare and present the annual budget. This would be based on departmental budgets drawn up by individual ministers and their officers which would be assembled by the Finance department for the consideration of the cabinet. Presentation to the legislature took place at about the end of February each year in the budget session, so that the bill of appropriation became law before the end of March and effective from the financial year starting on 1 April.

The budget provided for two main types of expenditure, the first representing the normal activities of government, in its day-to-day work, and the second, called 'the schedule of new expenditure' incorporating proposals for either new projects and services, or the expansion of old ones. An estimate of revenues was included in the budget, and taxation proposals were announced in the finance minister's speech.

The essential scrutiny of state expenditure was in principle meant to be performed through the budgetary procedure which in one way or another went on throughout the year with a concentrated push during the two months before the budget went to the legislature. For many reasons, however, the budget was not a meticulous, balanced, or final, picture of expenditure during the year. Individual ministers were apt to support and pass on to the Finance department all their proposals, irrespective of the funds likely to be available, with the result that when all these were put together, they invariably had to be drastically cut by the cabinet. This was done in a series of meetings where each minister, supported by his administrative experts, haggled with his colleagues for the largest amount he could get. At these budget meetings the finance secretary acted as secretary to the cabinet, whereas on all other occasions it was the chief secretary. The budget that emerged was a patchwork of last minute pressures and compromises so that the details had to be scrutinised *post facto* rather than beforehand. The source and quantity of finance available for several projects depended on allocation of funds by the centre. There was also frequent uncertainty about the quantity of foreign exchange that might be available and this was a vital factor, even when small, for many projects. Particular projects proceeded faster than others so that expenditure was often more or less than anticipated.

In these circumstances the examination of expenditure became a continuing process and the budget itself was a notional, necessarily time-bound, crystallization of the best informed projection of data at the time of presentation. It was an expression of intent rather than a strict plan of action. Changes were of course brought to the notice of the legislature for their approval in the supplementary demands made each autumn and again in the review and vote on revised estimates made with the annual budget. Many items in these revisions were presented at a stage where the legislature was powerless to take any effective action in the matter. Nevertheless as long as expenditure was directed to the purposes and works indicated in the budget, the legislature accepted this procedure as within the terms of its financial control.

The budget, more particularly the tax proposals, was regarded as secret up to the moment of their presentation. Secrecy was maintained by confining knowledge of tax proposals largely to the Finance minister and his secretary. These were discussed in confidence with the chief minister, who might on occasion consider one aspect or another in consultation with one or more of the other ministers. On the whole, however, the finance minister's budget speech would include elements of surprise for some of his colleagues.

Secrecy was generally hard to maintain in the state government. Information about cabinet discussions was often leaked and it would be difficult, at times even unwise, to trace the source, more often than not a minister himself. Secrecy when achieved was through a conspiracy of silence among the limited number of ministers and officials concerned.

The Finance department had also to watch and maintain the 'ways and means' position of the state, to ensure that current liabilities were honoured by money in the till. This could be quite a tricky job. Many sources of revenue were seasonal or periodic. Land revenue and the bigger irrigation dues were collected twice a year following the harvest. Fees from liquor licences, which became one of the largest sources of income in the Punjab, were operated on an annual basis. And so on. On the other hand most expenditure was continuous, for example on salaries and allowances paid monthly. 'Works' went on throughout the year, with possibly a hold-up of two to three months during the monsoon when rain made construction difficult. Many projects were financed by central loans, or even by smaller scale grants, many of them conditional. Regular accounting was therefore required to satisfy the centre and obtain a release of the funds due from them.

It is true that the state government was empowered to take loans from the Reserve Bank to meet its current needs, but beyond a small automatic cushion these had to be explained and justified in good time to be of effective use. The government was authorized also to float loans on the money market but here again, in view of the concentration of that market mostly in Bombay, state loans were largely directed both as to timing and quantity by guidance from the Reserve Bank.

The ways and means position required dual effort, on the one hand at making the most in good time of collecting internal revenues and central allocations through the many departments charged with this responsibility; and on the other hand of keeping the regulatory authority of the Reserve Bank fully informed regarding needs and obtaining its approval to meet these when necessary.

The Union government played a significant role in determining the quantum of expenditure by the state. The most vital and ambitious projects for development were often exclusively, or substantially financed by the centre. For bigger schemes which were almost invariably designed to be productive at least in the long term, central loans were made available. There were, however, other schemes which might be part loan and part grant, or initial grant and later transfer to state responsibility. A variety of patterns of central financing were developed. As most of this outlay related to the financing of the crucial additional development in the state budget, it inevitably introduced an element of influence and control, even the possibility of interference, by the central government.

These procedures produced the need for continuous liaison between the centre and the state through the specialist departments concerned and often involving the Finance department. The desire in the state was to have the largest possible budget for development, with the consequence that the centre was constantly and continuously being pursued and persuaded to allocate money for new proposals; any central schemes with financial assistance, even of a conditional kind, tended to be accepted readily by the state. The Punjab's largest project in the 1950s, the Bhakra Dam, with the related power and irrigation works, was financed by central loans. The state also readily accepted the community development project for rural areas, planned by the centre and financed initially by prescribed sharing with the states.

There was provision in the constitution for the appointment every five years of a commission to allocate a devolution of a portion of revenues from the centre to the states. These consisted mainly of shares of income tax and central excise duties. The president appointed the first Finance Commission at the end of 1951, with Mr K. C. Neogy as chairman. The periodic finance commissions were objects of interest and ingratiating attention by the states, which endeavoured to make out the strongest case for the largest allotment of finance.

In these many ways the state government was vitally linked with the centre for its development programmes, and in these arrangements the Planning Commission, established by the Union government in March 1950, soon came to play the dominant role. Through its advice for the allocation of central assistance to the states, and for particular projects, the Commission was able to direct planning and development operations and achieve its objectives. As it gained knowledge, experience, and strength, it became the main forum where the development schemes and expenditure of the state government were determined and the core of its budget prepared. The Commission was powerful, including in its membership both the Prime Minister, as chairman, and the Finance Minister of the Union. The deputy chairman, who was the whole-time chief of the Commission, was of ministerial rank and was frequently a member of the cabinet, holding the portfolio of Planning.

The Five Year Plan was the nation's blueprint for development, comprising as it did the centre's projects, those of each state and a broad outline of the extent and direction of investment for the private sector. Apart from this, however, the Commission, in consultation with the ministries concerned, became the clearing house for a great deal of the knowledge, statistics, and even technical operational details of major projects. The Punjab government had to refer constantly to it for approvals of all kinds, especially for foreign exchange. The Commission also developed the practice of an annual plan meeting, held usually in December, with the ministers and officers of the state involved, to allocate funds and define programmes for the coming financial year. As often as not the chief minister himself attended this meeting and the finance minister invariably did. Given the influence the Planning Commission enjoyed, and the specialized knowledge it developed, it was the operative arbiter of most of the government of India's development funds. These meetings with the Commission became more important, in the dispensing of finance, than the state's own cabinet. Financial outlays would be determined and priorities indicated which eventually found their way into the respective budgets of the Union and state governments. The pattern of finances laid down by the constitution, and as operated between the Union and the state, became an instrument and sanction for planning the economy under central direction.

The Punjab was launched on a programme of many-sided development which, backed by the hard work of its farmers particularly and
the people generally, soon made it the top state of independent India
in all-round economic progress. During this early period two projects
involved especially difficult administrative and coordinating problems:
Chandigarh and the Bhakra Dam.

Chandigarh, of which the population in the 1961 census was 99,000
and 219,000 in 1971, was started in 1951. The government first selected
the officer who would be responsible for its administration. This was
P. N. Thapar of the ICS, the senior financial commissioner in the state.
The chief administrator, as he was called, selected and the government
approved the appointment of Le Corbusier as the chief architect. Le
Corbusier chose Maxwell Fry and Jane Drew from the United Kingdom, and Pierre Jeanneret, a Swiss of French origin, as his team. A
group of Indian architects was selected with their assistance. The ideas
that developed in the architecture and construction of Chandigarh had
a profound influence and were imitated throughout India, particularly
in the North, including Delhi. This experience represents in fact a
turning away in India from the old pattern of the British regime where
buildings, with rare exceptions, were designed not by architects but by
engineers under the supervision of the Public Works Department.

Chandigarh was conceived and developed as a fully planned town,
to be financed partly from private and partly from public funds. The
residential buildings, except a limited number provided for ministers
and government employees, were to be privately owned. The plots
were laid out according to a master plan, and construction was subject
to the comprehensive bye-laws defined for the capital. The services and
amenities for the town, together with the buildings required for
government offices, were financed from public funds. The main
'capitol complex', including the nine-levelled secretariat, the High
Court, and the legislature, was designed by Le Corbusier himself.

The chief administrator supervised and coordinated the work of
three distinct, and substantially independent, branches dealing with
engineering and public health, architecture, and the estate office
responsible for the disposal of plots, accounting, and public relations.
Skilful team work and an atmosphere of mutual trust and frank
criticism was developed. The project achieved from its start a high
degree of efficiency, which brought a big response from the people in
investment in the future capital. Plots, which to start with were sold at
fixed prices, could soon be put on the open market, thereby increasing
project revenue to meet the financing of the city. Both the interest of
citizens, and success in stimulating good standards of performance and
maintenance, were furthered by providing forums where the public
could ventilate criticisms and express needs in open discussions on

construction plans, and could inspect models and specifications for residences.

The project was financed as far as government expenditure was concerned by central assistance, mostly in the form of loans. The bulk of the costs of development of the permanent utilities, such as the road and sewerage systems, were recovered in the sale price of plots, particularly those for commercial purposes which were invariably sold in open competition. The government, however, undertook to levy no local taxes for a period of twenty-five years ending in 1975.

While the architecture of Chandigarh has been controversial, attracting strong criticism and high praise, it is agreed that it is among the cleanest and best laid out cities in India. It has also satisfied the desire of the people of the Punjab for a centre for their state and culture. It has attracted investment, and is now well established also as an educational centre of importance. The roses grown in the 'Leisure Valley' of the city, which runs through its centre, are even exported to Europe during the winter.

As an administrative effort the project developed a well-earned reputation for the happy and constructive cooperation between the various elements that worked in it, and as an amicable and fruitful partnership between East and West.

Both technically and administratively the Bhakra Dam, with its connected irrigation and power works, was an even more ambitious venture. It is India's largest multi-purpose river valley scheme, and the dam is one of the biggest and most difficult constructions of its kind in the world. The idea, and a possible site for a dam on the River Sutlej, first occurred to Sir Louis Dane, Governor of the Punjab, when in the first decade of the century he was riding through the country near Bhakra. A file on the subject was then started, but the project was taken up only after independence. Construction started in 1951 and took over ten years to complete.

The main components of the project comprise a 226 metre high concrete dam across the River Sutlej at Bhakra; a 29 metre high dam at Nangal, some five miles lower; a 64 kilometre long Nangal Hydel Channel, across terrain broken up by hundreds of rain-fed torrents, the canal often carried above them, so as to allow the cross drainage of water below; four power stations, of which two are at Bhakra, one on each bank, and two at Gangowal and Kotla fed by the Nangal Hydel Channel; 1,104 kilometres of canals, and 3,360 kilometres of distributories. The storage capacity of the reservoir created by the Bhakra Dam, comprising a huge lake behind it, is 740,000 hectare metres. The canal system covers a gross area of 2,740,000 hectares, of which 2,370,000 are cultivated. The four power stations have an installed capacity of 1,204 MW.

There were several difficulties in undertaking these works. The benefits, and consequently the finance, were to be shared by at least three states, Punjab (in 1966 separated partly into Haryana), PEPSU (merged with Punjab in 1956) and Rajasthan. The gigantic lake created by the dam was to submerge villages not only of the Kangra district in Punjab but also of the princely state of Bilaspur (later merged in Himachal Pradesh) which indeed was to lose its capital of that name including the palaces of its ruling family and court. There was thus a human problem of some dimensions for the people who would lose their homes, and a matter of some delicacy as regards dealing with the influential families involved. Above all, technically the important works were outside India's experience. Much of the know-how, equipment, and crucial personnel would have to be imported. This situation presented real problems of control, economy, and efficiency.

A Bhakra Control Board was set up by agreement between the governments through the good offices of the centre. It comprised technical and financial representatives of the centre and the Punjab, and technical representatives of PEPSU and Rajasthan. At a later date a representative of Himachal Pradesh was associated with it in decisions about the problem of 'oustees', made homeless by the lake. It was agreed by all the governments that decisions of the Board would be accepted and implemented by each as if these were decisions of the government concerned. It was decided that the Governor of the Punjab should be chairman of the Board, and the head of the centre's irrigation and power commission, an engineer, should be its vice-chairman. Unity in command for construction was ensured by the decision that the Punjab should be in charge of constructing the dam and power stations, and that the ancillary canals and distributories would be constructed by the state governments in whose territories they lay.

These arrangements worked extraordinarily well. It will be noticed that they amounted to a self-abnegation ordinance by the governments concerned who, having created the Board, left it free from any interference in its work and undertook to honour its decisions. The technical and financial administration of the construction was thus insulated from politics. That these organizational arrangements worked efficiently and smoothly from the start was largely due to the work and capacity of the Board's first chairman, C. M. Trivedi, the Governor of the Punjab. He took meticulous pains in preparing the ground for controversial decisions, especially where they could have political repercussions. He realized that the politicians had kept themselves out of the affairs of this area's biggest project so that there might be untramelled construction, and he was careful to give them full explanations and consult them in advance of the Board's meetings, to make this arrangement effective and workable.

The Board was fortunate in selecting and being able to appoint Harvey Slocum from the USA as the construction superintendent for Bhakra Dam to work as a colleague of the Indian general manager. Slocum came to the country on a ten-year contract in his late fifties. A Texan, he had many of the reputed characteristics of that breed of men. A tireless worker, exacting taskmaster, a hard swearer, he was uncompromising on principle and unfailing in effort. At one time there were as many as a hundred foreigners, mostly Americans in view of their experience on dams, working for the project. This team was not only used to good effect on construction, but Slocum cooperated in ensuring that Indians were trained rapidly and relentlessly to replace them. Slocum unfortunately died in India during the course of his contract. He had however taken the dam to a stage where it was not necessary to replace him nor to delay its completion.

While Indian engineers had the theoretical knowledge, they often lacked practical experience, and there was the traditional aversion of the educated Indian to work with his hands. Both these difficulties were surmounted, and the project was not only able to dispense rapidly with most of the foreign personnel, but also to build up knowledge and establish confidence that, should India be called on to undertake a similarly complex work, it would be able to do so without foreign personnel.

In the projections made regarding the demand for electricity the project was caught on the wrong foot. The most optimistic estimates by experts suggested that supply would be in excess of demand, and the problem was met by the centre constructing at the same time the Nangal fertilizer factory to take off a big load of power at a concessionary price. The Punjab has lived to rue the decision; its own consumers have been short of electricity almost from the beginning. Slocum had advised that the government would find the demand far in excess of their estimates and in the event was proved correct.

In both the Chandigarh and the Bhakra projects Pandit Nehru played a significant role in relation to Le Corbusier and Slocum who had great personal faith in him and kept in touch with him. They were often at cross-purposes with the system of work in India, particularly the dilatory procedures of government decision-making. Slocum regularly threatened to resign. At many points of apparently no return it was the relationship Nehru had with these men that brought them back to the sweat of collaboration with the system and their Indian colleagues.

The Finance department also had the responsibility of advising on salaries of political office-holders, though the decisions made were at political level. These early years of independence saw the start of the practice, which has continued and grown, of low salaries for ministers and other political appointments, combined with perquisites which more than compensate. Congress came to power determined that in a poor country elected representatives of the people should receive a poor wage. The Punjab fixed its chief minister's salary at Rs 1500.00 per month with a sumptuary allowance of Rs 500.00, ministers at Rs 1500.00, and deputy ministers at Rs 800.00. As against these the highest paid ICS officer in the state received Rs 3500.00. Inevitably these wholly inadequate ministerial salaries became the justification for concessions in kind. Very soon political masters were enjoying facilities like rent-free housing, with furniture and a certain amount of what was in effect domestic service provided; free electricity and water; free transport, whether for public or private use; free telephones and medical facilities. In one way or another political appointments were in effect fully and even extravagantly 'nationalized', which is the term Bhim Sen Sachar used to describe his aim on this subject. This emphasis has prevailed and remains the operative influence in the Punjab and indeed throughout India. Ministers have thus become fully protected against inflation. Indeed whenever there is a crisis, political office-bearers lead the way in offering a cut in their salaries. An element of farce and an opportunity for abuse has continued in Indian political life in the hope of sustaining the public's illusion that their leaders work for a pittance. It is political office-bearers who can afford to send a chauffeur-driven car to the market should the family be in need of a pound of turnips.

6

RURAL MISSION, 1954-1957

On 2 October 1952, Mahatma Gandhi's birthday, India launched a gigantic organized effort for human welfare in its community development programme for its villages. There had been several experiments and efforts at rural improvement, including those associated with the work of F. L. Brayne particularly, and M. L. Darling, in the British period in the Punjab. Albert Mayer's Etawah project, after independence, had attracted interest, dedication, and work. But the community development programme sought, for the first time, to establish a national movement, and the necessary administration, to lift India's half million or more villages from poverty to the platform of scientific development and progress. It was designed as an avalanche which would sweep away before it the backlog of the past.

S. K. Dey, the minister for Community Development and Co-operation in the Union government (1956-65), had been associated with, and worked for, the idea of such a programme ever since independence. Before his appointment as minister he was the administrator for the programme. He became the driving force behind it and was able to stimulate and secure the blessings, patronage, and interest of Pandit Nehru.

Dey, a graduate of the University of Michigan, started his career as an executive of an American business house in India, and acquired much of his style, the pinpointed thrust and the gift and practice of aggressive salesmanship, from his experience. At independence, he threw up his business career and decided to put his future into the national effort to build up the country. He began by working as an engineer among the refugees displaced from Pakistan in northwest India, but soon went into politics. He adopted the appearance of a Congressman and dressed strictly according to the prescriptions of the party, usually in *khadi chust pajama* (close fitting pyjama of handspun cloth), a white flowing shirt, the Jawahar jacket, and Gandhi cap. He wore this 'uniform' with a bustling, almost bursting, energy and an aura of ideas and volubility. The caption, 'son of a farmer', adorned his office door at Nilokheri in the Punjab, where he organized his first effort at community building.

He claimed to have selected Nilokheri, some sixty-five miles from Delhi, for its inhospitable terrain, as a challenge to establish a township on sheer will. The site was well served with communications, lying between the main railway line and the Grand Trunk Road, but had little else to recommend it. Here Dey organized a community of refugees with a mixed agricultural and urban economy. This entirely synthetic township has survived and is today a moderately well-off urban area with a rural fringe. Dey expended great skill in manipulation to attracting patronage, including a large printing unit set up by the central government.

Two other men were closely associated with establishing the community development idea. V. T. Krishnamachari, the deputy chairman of the Planning Commission, laboured hard at propagating the use of the cooperative society as the economic institution for rural improvement. Dr Douglas Ensminger, the representative of the Ford Foundation, lived and worked in India for almost two decades. He wrote a handbook for the movement, a drill-master's precise detail of exercises and a prophet's aspirations, called *A Guide to Community Development*, which was put out in January 1957, with a foreword by Dey, and a revised edition appeared in March 1962.

The programme was directed towards bringing to the people in the villages the experience of applying modern science and its methods to their economic occupations and their way of living. It was not directed at them but *through* them. They were to be provided with the means to experiment with, see for themselves, and make part of their life experience, the methods which modern knowledge could make available for their self-propagating, snow-balling, progress. It was not a plan for regimentation, but one for enabling people to discover, and multiply, the ways to the good life. Said Dey:

. . . experiences in different parts of the world confirm that poverty can be eradicated and wealth created in its place. However, it remains yet to be proved that physical well-being for man can co-exist with the freedom and dignity of his spirit . . . Democracy will not survive if it cannot find a living answer to this basic question. Community Development in India is an all-out quest for this answer.

The instrument of change and development was knowledge brought to the village and imbibed in experience within it. This would then become the means of self-reliant progress and recurring vistas of spiralling aspiration and achievement. Known and familiar institutions were earmarked to achieve this end: the village community, the co-operative society, and the school. Community development sought to strengthen these organizations, so that they should become the means of discovering the needs of the community and of making the corporate effort to achieve them. Stress was laid on attention to securing the interest and the work of women as the essential lever for improvements in the home, and for the nurture, growth, and vision of youth and the coming generations.

The institutional expression of the village community was the *panchayat* (literally a council of five, though numbers were not limited to this figure). It is difficult to discover clearly when and to what extent the *panchayat* of the past was a live entity for action in the village, but there is no doubt that the idea of the *panchayat*, as a self-governing village body, remained an affectionate and respected symbol in historical memory and tradition. It is this that explains its mention in the Indian constitution, which provides a 'Directive Principle' for their development. At independence *panchayats* were legally constituted bodies in most states, including the Punjab. The community development programme sought to use this institution, known to the village, as the main instrument of development.

The cooperative society was to be the organization for business, to provide credit, equipment, and the farmer's inputs. The cooperative movement started in the Punjab in 1904 when the Cooperative Credit Societies Act was passed, and it had made progress that was sound though patchy in coverage.

Traditionally the school-teacher had always been held in respect as a man apart, the repository of learning and dedicated to it and to a way of life that held the best of India's spiritual heritage. Much change had, however, taken place in his position over the years, and frequently his indigence of circumstance and opportunity was such that it was difficult to recognize in him either learning or spirituality. Nevertheless the idea of the teacher as a source of light persisted as a myth of the land. There was an increased and insistent demand for education following independence and thus a base for the belief that the village school could be turned to use for improvement and progress.

The agency, supplied by the government to bring modern knowledge and practices to the village, was called the National Extension Service. After some preliminary experimenting starting in 1952, the 'block' came to be recognized and enforced as the uniform area organization. It was planned as a group of about one hundred villages, with a population of 60,000 to 80,000, and was headed by a block development officer. By virtue of pay, qualifications, and experience the block development officer would rank in the third line of the generalist administrative services, after the ICS/IAS and the state civil service. He was to lead the team of officials who were required to maintain intimate contact with the village and bring to it the knowledge and organization required to meet its defined needs and potentialities for development, economic and human. The block development officer's team would get their know-how from the specialized departments of the government. It was to be a two-way traffic, ideas and requirements thrown up from the village, with knowledge and the means of their realization provided by specialists, in each case through the block development officer.

The official in immediate contact with the village was the village level worker, in charge of ten villages. He was of about the same rank as a village accountant (*patwari*) of the revenue agency. He was an all-purpose worker, to be trained and experienced to communicate, in simple form, information and methods relevant to the various items of development desired by the village.

Between the block development officer and the village level worker, and attached to the former's staff as his subordinates, were usually six specialized extension workers for agriculture (usually a graduate); animal husbandry; cooperation and *panchayats*; social education (one man and one woman); and simpler forms of construction such as culverts, street-paving, and the repair of wells (an overseer of the Public Works department). These were 'the carriers of know-how', of a rank which may be generally classed as 'inspector', the lowest operative executives in their line. It was recognized that these extension officers could not meet all the needs that might arise but at this stage, no doubt to limit expenditure, it was decided that other specialized help (for example for small industry) should be obtained from the normal area staffs of the departments.

With an 'accountant cum storekeeper', a clerk, and three 'Grade IV employees' (in fact messenger peons) the personnel for the block development officer was complete. In addition, however, each block was supplied with a jeep and a driver, to ensure mobility in what was a fairly small area, on the average 600 square kilometres. The provision of public motor transport for a unit of this size was unusual, and indicated the priority and urgency which the government attached to the work. Two unkind comments arose from the envy that such transport provoked in other branches of the administration. One was that the jeep was a means by which the United States, which supported and assisted the programme, ensured the supply of American equipment to India. Secondly, the organization came to be dubbed 'the department of jeeps and keeps', implying that the jeep was also used for activities of an amorous nature not listed among the scheduled achievements of the block.

The district officer was assigned a crucial role in the community development movement. All the blocks in the district were under his charge and he was responsible not only for coordinating supplies and services required by them but for acting as the leader of the team of all the district's specialized agencies so as to maintain and improve the flow of knowledge, guidance, inspection, and supervision.

The overall policy and personnel control lay with the secretary of the department, with the rank of a commissioner, who worked directly under the minister for the subject at state headquarters. He had authority to supervise the activities of all the heads of department to achieve the common objectives of the programme. He was also in charge of all the normal secretarial functions of a department, including budgeting, law, training, and recruitment policy. The apex of the organization was the Ministry of Community Development (to which was added in 1958 the additional responsibility and title, 'and Co-operation'). It was from here that the philosophy, the overall financial and training arrangements, as also much of the jargon that the movement developed, were produced and disseminated.

This system ran from Delhi to the four corners of the country and each year from 1952 onwards covered added blocks in each state until all the villages of India were included. Supporting it were specialized servicing units, some of them in every state, others limited to serve several, for the training of personnel at all levels of the organization, from schools for village level workers to the National Institute for Community Development set up at Hyderabad, which not only trained and stimulated the most senior executives, including collectors and commissioners, but also undertook investigation and research programmes.

The movement was supported by an all-India pattern of finance. This took the form of heavy central assistance, amounting to a good 75 per cent of the expenditure, and tapering off after ten years to routine administrative activity provided mostly by the state. The budget for each block was drawn up as Stage I for the first five years, and Stage II for the subsequent five. The provision for the former was 12 lakhs (Rs 1,200,000) and for Stage II, 5 lakhs (Rs 500,000). The higher allotment in the first period was on the assumption that initially villages would have to be introduced to and made interested in the whole idea of self-help. Funds were therefore provided not only to cover the cost of staff and administration but for schemes of village improvement, agricultural development and other amenities, most of which were financed partly by the government and partly by the beneficiaries. At Stage II it was hoped that the villages would be sufficiently aroused to finance local improvements themselves and the budget was accordingly limited substantially to administrative expenses.

The community development programme was sold to the states on the basis of the large financial assistance provided. Not that the states were averse to the principle; quite the contrary, most of them welcomed it. But if central assistance had not been available it is likely they would have adopted varying patterns of effort for village development; a uniform all-India scheme would not have emerged. The large expenditure involved also led to the introduction of blocks in each state by instalments, designed to be completed by 1963, but in fact achieved to cover the whole country somewhat later. In the Punjab,

Dey visited the state to sell the idea to Bhim Sen Sachar in 1952. It was clear from the discussion of it that this consultation was a formality and courtesy, as the programme had already received the blessings of the central government and was being advanced with the whole weight of its influence.

The community development movement produced a buzz of activity in the villages, which were constantly prodded and provoked to effort. It received the attention of the government at all levels, from the village to Delhi. VIPs visited the more promising areas. The Punjab, on the doorstep of Delhi, received considerable attention and both the Shah of Iran and Bulganin and Khruschev inspected villages in the state. The Russian leaders attracted a great deal of interest and were described by villagers, who flocked in thousands to see them, as representing *garibon ke sarkar* (a government of the poor).

There was inevitably a considerable emphasis on manifest performance. Both officials and people wanted to 'see' things happening. The most obvious achieved priority. The cleaning and paving of village streets, the construction of smoke-free kitchens, the performance of women and children in song, dance, and drama, the cleaning of wells, and the planting of trees became daily events, the activities faithfully enumerated in the block development officer's pro forma of 'achievements'. There was a good response from the villages who provided their share of effort, or money, or land to attract the conditional grants which were a feature of many of the schemes in the block budget.

It is doubtful, however, whether the movement produced any deep impact in regard to the improvement of experience with reference to economic activity and ways of living. An entirely new activity seemed to do better than an improvement or a fundamental change in the old. Thus modern poultry farming was introduced from scratch to Punjab villages and was so successful that the big egg drove out, in a few years, the *desi* ('native') small one. The Punjab was soon supplying eggs and meat well beyond its borders, particularly to the large consumer market in Delhi, at prices so attractive that the consumption of these foods spiralled.

But where modern methods of scientific production required a change in traditional attitudes and ways, no impact of any dimensions was achieved. The Punjab is burdened, though less so than other parts of India, with considerable numbers of useless cattle. Hindu veneration of the cow prohibits its slaughter. Aged, ill, and starving cattle were often let loose on the countryside, driven from place to place by individual farmers protecting their crops. Villages, even at a considerable distance from the Pakistan border, would often urge that the police should be requested to close their eyes to the passage of cattle into Pakistan. The object of this request was clear. The cattle must not, because of the religious taboo, be killed and used in India; if they went to Pakistan, everybody knew they would be eaten but they would not burden the conscience of the Punjabi farmer.

Nor was there evidence of manifest change in methods of farming. It is doubtful if the programme provided the meticulous detailed package of knowledge and of inputs which scientific farming required. An American extension worker—and some were provided for assistance in the Punjab—visiting a village would usually avoid the festive gathering in the residential area, and proceed to the farmer's fields. He would go round and point out a defect here, a possible improvement there, each usually related to a specific act or a required input. He would occasionally praise a particular effort. The programme as a whole, however, lacked this kind of detailed expertise related to the needs of particular fields. This is not surprising. The mass contact man of the movement was the village level worker. He generally had no experience of practical agriculture. He was meant to be fed by the scientific experts of the specialized departments. But most of the agricultural extension officers also lacked practical experience. The result was that much of the effort was hit or miss, providing generalities of prescription and good behaviour for scientific farming, rather than the detailed diagnosis applicable to the particular soil, and the practical availability of the inputs of material and labour that it needed. The expertise available was not expert enough.

The programme did not seem to strike at the centre of its defined objective, which was to produce a true marriage of minds and practice between the cultivator and the knowledge of farming that would manifestly improve both his experience and his production. It remained largely a movement initiated and pushed from the top rather than one which took root in the habits and desires of the people it sought to serve. Unlike the food administration set up from scratch from 1943 onwards (considered in Chapter 3) community development was never stretched to accurate, measurable targets of performance. Its objectives remained many-faceted and general, and were not crystallized into recognizable forms of controlled activity, yielding manifest results. It remained, in many ways, an exercise of goodwill rather than of better production or better living for its clientele.

Could more have been achieved in a different way? A great deal of effort and expenditure was directed to creating a mass contact agency for the village. The government already had an administrative set-up, in the revenue agency, with tentacles of mass contact in each village. From the *patwari* (village accountant), through the *tehsil*, and up to the collector the hierarchy had functioned for several decades. Could not this agency with some degree of modification and strengthening have performed the mass contact function? It would have had to be fed with knowledge and trained, but that was true of the village level worker and the block development officer also. Such an arrangement was discussed and rejected at policy level. The government took the view that the revenue hierarchy was conservative, rigid with age, unadaptive to the new, with the appearance and air of past authoritarianism. It felt it could neither be used as it was utilized nor adjusted to new objectives or wider horizons.

If expenditure had been saved on the mass contact agency, more would have been available for the crucial need, expertise, organized at a much higher level of knowledge and practicality. The extension work required to meet the practical needs of the village was of a meticulous quality. The expertise might well have done infinitely better if spread much thinner in quantity and much thicker in knowledge. One or two highly educated and experienced agricultural experts for the district might have given far more practical guidance than a graduate for each block. The Punjab later achieved tremendous results in agricultural production partly through the association of the Agricultural University, set up by Kairon at Ludhiana, with the needs of its farmers.

The general purpose supervisor, the block development officer, was also conceived at too low a level of education and performance. His crucial task was to discover what potential was available in his villages, from the point of view of both material possibilities and the human response to them, and to get assistance in the way of applicable methods and resources to the people. He had to formulate the questions that the experts should consider and answer, and to communicate the answers to his clients. This was no small job if properly performed. A more highly educated and experienced executive was required, particularly one who could discriminate between the spurious and impractical and identify the essential elements which could produce manifest advantage. A way out would have been to have a sub-divisional officer in each *tehsil*. The Punjab had these appointments in selected areas as part of the general administrative structure. These were invariably either young officers of the ICS/IAS or older ones from the state civil service, in both cases much more educated and experienced than the block development officer. An executive of this calibre could perhaps have defined both the questions that needed answers, and helped the two-way process of accurate knowledge between village and expert. A sub-divisional officer, with his development responsibilities given the highest emphasis, and his other administrative duties concerned with revenue and the law reduced, would have provided more effective, practical supervision both in ascertaining what the villages required and ensuring that they got their answers in sufficient practical detail, sometimes perhaps even frank negatives when knowledge or resources were not available. The general administrative duties and powers of the sub-divisional officer could have been used to support his development efforts. The fact that a *tehsil* was usually an area covering three to five blocks need not have diluted the quality of the supervision as it was compact enough to get to know in detail, particularly with the help of a jeep for transport.

Nor could the collector be expected to provide the concentrated administrative leadership of the movement. His association with it, in view of the overall coordinating powers and authority he enjoyed, was essential, but his duties were multifarious and the demands on his time eccentric and constant. He could not give concentrated attention to the detailed needs of development in groups of villages. His help could, however, have been invaluable, at crucial points in the process, provided he had the well-informed and educated assistance that a sub-divisional officer could have given.

Functional experts, working under the supervision of a not very experienced generalist, the block development officer, were apt to be used for a general impact on the village rather than for applying the knowledge and experience of their specialization to the practical needs of the village.

Altogether the movement was conceived and directed in terms of quantity. The results it strove to harvest properly demanded rigorous standards of practical quality. These were achieved only in chancy patches. Precision is the exacting and uncompromising raw material of science; the programme did not achieve this.

Nevertheless any categorical adverse judgement could not be proven. The Punjab, after independence, and more especially after 1967, made a great leap forward in agricultural production. Symptomatic of the change is the Ludhiana district which attained the all-world record in wheat yields, as reported in FAO Statistics (January to December 1971, volume 20 (1-12)). As against 33.10 quintals per hectare in Ludhiana, the Indian average was 12.1 and the American 20.9. Today the Punjab produces a quarter of India's total wheat production, and the Punjab and Haryana between them contribute a surplus of some millions of tonnes to the country. It is difficult to disentangle the influences that have produced these results. Did the community development programme help? Was it the Agricultural University? Was it the displaced farmer who put energy and determination to building his new farm? Was it the drive for change, seized and spurred on by Partap Singh Kairon, which is discussed in the next chapter? Was it the varieties of high-yielding seeds? Was it the taxation structure, which diverted money and even men at high levels from urban incomes to the lightly taxed investment in land? Many other factors could also be listed and it would be difficult to exclude any of them from a considered view. Dr

Douglas Ensminger's assessment of 1962 puts the problem from another angle:

In essence the Community Development Programme has as its objective the development of India's most precious resources—the village people . . .
Physical targets can be said to represent only the achievement of activities which may or may not be in the interest of the basic objective of the programme . . .
The most important of the Community Development objectives, however, is the long-range objective of firmly laying the foundations for the growth of a new village culture. A village culture in which the *panchayats*, the cooperatives and the village schools are strong and effective in guiding the people in finding solutions to their problems. Achieving the larger objective requires time—the spread over a generation, like the growing of a forest, the seeds of which are sown as part of the short-term programme.

Nor can there be any doubt of stupendous change in the Punjab village in the quarter century following independence. A glance at the wheat crop in January, when it is still green, reveals field after field of closely grown plants, so thick and regular one could almost walk on its solid mass. The variations in height have disappeared, as also the bald patches between plants. In the village, apart from bicycles that abound, are sewing machines, transistors, tractors, harvesters, motorcycles, and even jeeps. A great deal has changed and there are indications that a great deal will follow. Nor is the prosperity limited to one class. It is almost impossible to get labour in the Punjab, particularly during the harvesting season. In towns especially, in villages more often than not, labour from other states is employed, and flattered and cajoled to remain.

The trend and emphasis of the community development movement in the Punjab could well have been changed had one of the 'might have beens' of administrative history in the state been translated into fact. Early in 1955 a proposal was worked out in detail and approved by the state cabinet in March of that year, to convert the programme to implementation by local government institutions. It had the blessings and the keen interest of Bhim Sen Sachar, the chief minister.

The scheme aimed at setting up *tehsil* councils, comprising elected representatives from each block, voted for by the members of the village *panchayat*, thus providing a link between the village, through the block to the subdivision of the district. While the chairman of the council would be a non-official, elected by it, it would have the sub-divisional officer, who would be appointed in every *tehsil*, as its chief executive officer. He, along with the block development officers, would be members of the council. In this way while the non-official elected representatives would predominate they would have the direct support of officials. The community development programme would be administered by the *tehsil* council, and the block staffs would be placed squarely under their administrative control, though the government would continue to be responsible for recruitment and training. The council would enjoy defined powers of taxation and conditional upon its using these would be allocated, in addition to the block budget, ten per cent of the land revenue and irrigation dues collected in its area. The ultimate objective was that these sources of revenue would progressively be transferred for local use by local rural self-government organizations.

Above the *tehsil* council there would be a district council (*zilla parishad*) comprising representatives from the *tehsil* council, elected by it from the members, and a strong official element, including the subdivisional officers and representatives of the technical departments of the district, with the deputy commissioner as the *ex officio* chairman. This official texture was justified on the ground of functions, the proposal being that the executive implementing authority should be the *tehsil* council; the district council would be limited strictly to coordinating, supervisory, and regulatory functions, with no powers of taxation and no responsibility for administration except through the *tehsil* councils.

The whole scheme was designed to transfer initiative from the government to a viable authority representing the *panchayats*, operating in an area small enough to secure intimate knowledge and mobility, yet large enough for some degree of manoeuvre in the collection of finances and the selection of development projects of substantial benefit. This local authority was to have a basic budget provided by the government, with powers to enlarge this by taxation and a nucleus of staff, administrative and technical, headed by the sub-divisional officer, a high-level and educated officer.

These recommendations met with considerable opposition from the interests concerned. MLAs generally took the view that they should be *ex officio* members of the councils for their areas, whereas the government had decided that elected representatives should come in under their own steam, and not as emanations from another forum. The official machine expressed apprehension at serving directly under councils at *tehsil* level and felt it would become a plaything of local politics and pressures. The Ministry of Community Development reacted unfavourably to the thought of surrendering their budget and staff under controls which might ignore the heart of their programme. They also did not like the idea of the crucial executive unit being at the *tehsil* rather than the block level. Argument and debate went the rounds on these and other points. The scheme, which the Punjab cabinet had intended to implement from Gandhi's birthday anniversary on 2 October 1955 was delayed. There is little doubt, however, that it would have gone through, possibly on an experimental basis and with some compromises, were it not for the leadership contest between Sachar and Kairon, which diverted the former, who was fully behind the proposal, to a struggle for his own existence as chief minister. He was thrown out of power in January 1956 and the scheme was put on the shelf. Partap Singh Kairon had other priorities in mind.

At this stage it might be useful to digress briefly as to how a scheme of this kind originated in the government decision-making process and the broad stages through which it passed. When the community development programme was proposed to the Punjab through Dey in 1952 to Sachar as chief minister, one view, taken by the state finance secretary, was that it was best to provide a high level officer of the ICS/IAS or a senior man from the state civil service at each *tehsil* to supervise it. This would be a sub-divisional officer. The finance secretary had worked as a famine officer in 1940-41 and had seen how effectively an area of the size of a *tehsil* could be catered for in famine relief, by a sub-divisional officer type of man from the top civil service. In 1952, however, the programme emerged, pushed by the influence of the Union, in the form already described. By 1954-55 considerable experience had been gained and there was a degree of dissatisfaction in the Punjab that the programme was possibly not fulfilling its aims of arousing interest and developing experience among the villagers themselves, nor resulting in a manifest improvement in agricultural methods. In these circumstances Sachar was keen that the government should take a second look at it to see whether it could be better adapted to meet these aims. The idea was then put by the planning secretary briefly to the other secretaries concerned, including the financial commissioner, the secretaries for Community Development, Local Government, Finance and Law. Their initial reactions were obtained, and a more detailed proposal, making adjustments for points raised by them, worked out by the planning secretary. This was then commented on by the secretaries mentioned, and a series of discussions organized. Some of these discussions included selected executives, such as the commissioner of one division, and a few collectors. The proposal was then put to the chief minister in his portfolio of Planning, and approved for presenting to the state cabinet. At this stage the other secretaries concerned were formally consulted, but as the whole idea had already been thrashed out with them, and they in turn had discussed it with their colleagues and ministers, this last consultation was very brief. A memorandum then went to the cabinet and the proposal was approved with some minor changes of detail. Normally this should have completed the process of decision-making, but during the course of the build-up of the proposal, aspects of it had apparently been discussed with some of the MLAs who expressed interest particularly in regard to their representation in the councils. Sachar thought that it was advisable before finally going ahead with the scheme to consult representative MLAs and also obtain the reactions of the Ministry of Community Development. The scheme, as approved by the cabinet, was then printed and consultations took more time than had been anticipated. Meanwhile reactions among officials, particularly those whose services would be placed under the councils, had also been expressed and conveyed to both their hierarchical superiors and the interested ministers.

This process of decision-making, in the present case finally resulting in dropping a scheme to which considerable thought and discussion had been given, is fairly typical of administrative procedures in the Punjab at the time. The same type of processing would occur in other cases considered by the secretariat, varying from matters where the subject was considered simple enough for final decision by an officer, or his minister, to others, such as this scheme, where consultation included several departments of government, through their officers and ministers, and eventually the state cabinet. In this case it was also obvious that concerned interests, not directly responsible for the final decision, operated in making their views or reactions known to the decision-makers, and exerted influence on the final outcome.

The idea of the Punjab scheme, however, returned through another forum and by other means, though without any acknowledgement of its origins. This was possibly just as well, since what was eventually put through differed in crucial principle and detail, and in particular failed to insist on a firm transfer of responsibility and initiative to the local bodies. In 1957 the Balwantrai Mehta Committee, set up by the Government of India to examine various aspects of the community development programme, recommended what they called 'democratic decentralization'. While they left details to be worked out by each state, the proposal amounted to the idea that above the village *panchayat* the programme should now be associated with local government institutions formed by indirect elections from the *panchayats*. The National Development Council, the highest authority on development questions, including the Prime Minister as chairman and chief ministers among its members, endorsed the Balwantrai Mehta recommendation on 12 January 1958, amid resounding acclaim and publicity. The community development programme and the national extension service were thus transformed into what was called *panchayati raj* (the rule of the *panchayats*).

Panchayati raj was inaugurated in the Punjab (after several other states, Rajasthan being the first, had already done so), on Gandhi's birthday anniversary on 2 October 1962. The scheme placed the operative unit at the block through a *panchayat samiti*, and the senior body at the district. MLAs were made *ex officio* members of the councils where their constituencies lay. Block staff were to assist the councils but were not under their full administrative control. The idea of a sub-divisional officer was dropped.

The councils thus established in the Punjab have not created any great impression. They have been regarded as part of the paraphernalia of state level, rather than local, politics. Even the election process has been a matter of convenience at the will of the state government. After those held in 1964 there were none until 1972 in Punjab and Haryana.

From April 1969, central assistance to the community development programme was merged in the lump sum financial aid earmarked for the state, and no longer calculated per block.

With these changes, the process of decentralization and diversification was intensified. Varying practices have emerged in the states. The community development programme, as originally conceived on a uniform all-India pattern, has disappeared. It has now been taken over in various ways, and with differences of organization, priorities, and emphasis by the many forms of *panchayati raj* in the states.

7

CHIEF MINISTER PARTAP SINGH KAIRON

Partap Singh Kairon dominated the scene in the Punjab while he was chief minister from January 1956 to June 1964. He enjoyed unrivalled power and by reason of character, temperament, and work exercised almost exclusive direction of the administration. Born in 1901, he was not an educated man in any obvious sense. He could not sustain a cool, objective argument; he could, however, illumine and press his point of view with experience, confidence, and wit. He had many of the characteristics of the educated mind. He did not believe in or practise any kind of superstition, nor did he submit in form or action to tradition. His mind was unencumbered with the past. He was impatient to discover and apply the new. His formative years had been greatly influenced by ten years in the United States where at the age of eighteen he had gone to avoid possibly unpleasant notice from the British authorities following the Jallianwala Bagh tragedy, during which he had aroused their suspicion as a potentially violent rebel. Kairon worked on farms and in factories in the United States and saved enough to study for a degree from the University of Michigan. He was a strong believer in science as an instrument of change, and was invariably attracted by a new idea, even a gadget of practical or productive use. He worked hard himself and insisted that the Punjab, its administration, and its people should work also.

Kairon, a Jat himself, had many of the qualities and prejudices of the soldier-farmer tradition. He had strong and uncompromising loyalties. His attitude to Nehru was that of complete acceptance, of touching, even humble, faith, concern, and service, though there was little in common between them. His allegiance was fixed, practical, and unwavering. He also had a formidable and determined enmity for opponents, or those who roused his suspicions, or challenged his power. He had a strong sense of family loyalty and aspects of this with respect to his wife, his sons, and their friends eventually helped to erode and destroy his power.

This was truly like a man from fiction, dynamic, hard driving, passionate, and containing the many contradictions of his character and circumstances in a gigantic, overwhelming belief that destiny had chosen him as the instrument for change and progress. He drove himself, the public service, and the people to endeavour in every direction.

Kairon seized the Punjab as an arena for all-round development. He had been a minister continuously since 1947, and was already in intimate touch with the personnel of the services and the problems and people of the state. He harried and bullied the administration to move faster with the projects in operation and to start on several new ones. He devoted his attention to all classes of the population, particularly the Harijans, landless labourers, and women. He speeded up and completed the consolidation of holdings in the Punjab, a measure which enabled farmers to devote concentrated attention to their land; on this base was achieved the vast increase in agricultural production in the later 1960s. Within the consolidation programme he insisted that land should be earmarked for Harijan and labour housing, for schools and village amenities and services. He directed his departments towards increased employment of women and endeavoured to provide for the security required by them at their work.

Nor did Kairon ignore institutional improvements. He helped to found and build the Agricultural University at Ludhiana as well as the Postgraduate Research Institute for medicine at Chandigarh. He imposed a cess on the land revenue for limited periods which was allocated to improve standards of university education. This resulted in an expansion particularly of Kurukshetra University located in the Haryana region. Several public schools were started, with scholarships provided to help promising children from poorer families.

Even Kairon's most determined detractors concede that he contributed in every possible way to the development and economic progress of the Punjab. He provided a tremendous fillip to gearing up administration and people to processes and projects of economic change and improvement and to the discovery of the potentialities and the difficulties of applying modern scientific methods especially to the agricultural economy. While it is difficult to identify the exact contribution made by these ways of thinking and action to the tremendous growth in production achieved by the Punjab after Kairon's time, there seems small doubt that they created a climate for these results.

His methods of work and the means he utilized for the maintenance and consolidation of power had a profound influence on the administration. This chapter is concerned more with these means than with the development programmes he pursued. The system of work in government had thus far continued broadly as during the British period, although its content and variety had increased. The normal procedure was that a letter or problem, however it may have originated, was 'dealt with' at the Secretariat by the 'branch' concerned with it. The 'Paper Under Consideration', as it was called, was put up, with the record, indicating 'previous papers', 'policy', and 'precedent', if any, for an officer's orders. This started the process of 'noting', where the officer would either make orders on the case, or submit his views with the facts to his superior. Notings might often travel up to the minister or between departments, even between ministers, depending on the nature of the question to be decided. In complicated cases, or where new policy seemed to be involved, or where there were different views in the departments, the case might go not only to the chief minister, but even to the cabinet on the basis of a 'memorandum' with the facts and arguments. The 'notings' were the crucial hub of the decision-making process. They were confidential as between officers and ministers, and the pros and cons of action and its possible repercussions were fully and frankly discussed, so that the decision finally made should have taken account of all the implications. The officer dealing with a case was required to discover and point out all the relevant facts but was free to record such opinion as he had in regard to the implications of the various alternatives which he thought possible. He was required to obtain the opinion of other departments concerned should these be relevant and present a whole case to his superiors.

There had been changes in the atmosphere and context in which this system functioned since independence. Government activity had expanded, the secretariat had absorbed comparatively junior officers to meet its needs, and many of the ministers had little administrative experience. In these circumstances notings tended sometimes to lack the practical judgement which they had previously had. Nor was the strict, though necessarily at times somewhat broad, line of demarcation between policy and administration, which the secretariat had observed, so faithfully followed. With popular ministers heading the secretariat, it was inevitable that the public should push individual cases, and particularly complaints, with the ministers, and that at times in dealing with these the line between policy for the secretariat to determine and action for the executive to administer, should be blurred. Nevertheless on the whole the system continued to function within the terms prescribed for it.

In the secretariat system the chief secretary played, at official level, the crucial role. He was the secretary to the council of ministers and thus concerned with the supervision of all material prepared by the departments which required the orders of government at the highest level. It was his responsibility to ensure that the problems put to the council had been dealt with in the required detail and that, where more than one department was concerned, a properly coordinated view of the subject had been taken. The chief secretary was the personnel adviser to the chief minister, and directly in charge of the ICS/IAS and the state civil service (called the PCS). He also advised the chief minister and council on all matters which concerned the general conditions of service of all the departments. He dealt with the staffing problems of the ministers' offices, and generally with the administration as a whole for matters where politics touched on it. To perform these functions the chief secretary had special powers, permitting for example access to the files of all the departments, and opportunity to bring problems to the notice of ministers and if necessary for the overall orders of the chief minister. Needless to say, many of these powers were better unexercised, assumed to exist in reserve, not pushed to definition. Much good government as far as a chief secretary went lay in prevention and anticipation rather than in control; in adjustments and whittling down of differences and frictions rather than in their exposure for the orders of superior authority.

To this system of work Kairon administered a series of shocks, especially with regard to the sources from which he obtained information and the direct working contacts he established with both members of the public and individual officials. Temperamentally he was compulsive in making himself available for information at all levels. He was unwilling, indeed perhaps incapable, of waiting for a problem to climb up the executive and secretariat ladder to the minister's table. The paper under consideration thus began to erupt from all kinds of causes, a telephone call from one of his 'men' in the districts, a story from an official, a discussion in cabinet, an idea thrown out by a visitor. Nor was he inclined to wait for such problems to be docketed in the relevant office and come up the line with tabulated data and notings. A great deal of business was transacted across the table, and the chief minister would often indicate a stance or posture, even issue an order, before the bureaucratic machine had the opportunity to sift the grain from the chaff.

This tendency brought its inevitable consequences. People took great pains to gain the chief minister's ear in the knowledge that he was willing, often eager, to listen. The habit of carrying tales to the highest executive snowballed. People tried to push problems up higher and higher so that these might be considered at the chief minister's forum. Officials often had to tender advice, or at least reaction, without adequate opportunity to ascertain the facts or assess the consequences. Intermediate authorities all along the line tended to get cut out of the decision-making process and to feel that decisions, which sometimes proved faulty or unfair, had been thrust on them, impairing both initiative and a sense of responsibility. Some officials too were quick to take advantage of such a situation. Direct access to the chief minister now appeared to be the target. Kairon's provincial transport controller, for example, was seen as a man who had achieved easy access to him, so his help was sought, in all manner of ways, for redress or patronage.

Other officers modelled themselves in this image. The moderate, the sound, and cautious lost ground and confidence. Partap Singh Kairon no doubt was largely inspired by the zeal for action; he wished to make a breakthrough, to eliminate red tape, to get on with the job. These methods however were differently assessed by his public and most of his officials. They made it possible for people to believe that they were used to extend his personal power, and for ambitious officials to feel that this was a means to enhance their own influence and importance.

In this situation Kairon's family soon became the target for criticism. His wife and two sons, Surrinder Singh and Gurrinder Singh, were accused of using his power as a means of acquiring wealth for their business. The Punjab was riddled with stories of the misuse of influence for family fortunes. This became a weapon for use by all the political forces, individual and corporate, that opposed Kairon's power; they succeeded in the end in overthrowing him.

The result was that even in the heyday of Kairon's authority, the 'system' worked in a fury of activity, up and down and across the lines, with Kairon inextricably and invariably mixed up in it at all levels. The whole government was driven by the will and inexhaustible energy of the chief minister into doing what was immediately necessary on the vast number of matters brought to its notice, and then clearing up and sorting out the elements of the cases into some degree of order to meet the requirements of law, finance, rule, and procedure. A daily task for Kairon's administration was to adapt the chief minister's urges and policy to the requirements of a rule of law.

Nor did Kairon enjoy the benefits of restraint by the corporate influence of his cabinet. They were dependent on his power, with the mass of voters solidly behind him. In 1961 he threw out Rao Birendra Singh, the influential minister of Revenue from the Haryana area, by a dismissal order passed by the Governor. In 1962 another colleague, the previous chief minister of PEPSU, Gian Singh Rarewala, was induced to resign. Kairon's restraints and moderation were entirely self-generated and minimal. Politically he did not need caution, temperamentally it did not suit him.

Yet it would be incorrect to conclude that he was constantly involved with the task of struggling through a morass of disorder and opposition. He struck a chord and a rhythm with the people, and during his peak period of power carried the action before him, without hindrance or hesitation, indeed even with acclaim and devotion. So fearless and uncompromising was his leadership that within his own time of supreme power he faced with equal lack of concern the consequences of the disrepair to the system and the revenge of the many enemies he had treated with contempt.

The influence of Kairon's methods of work and exercise of power may now be considered with reference to certain branches of the administration and its institutions. Kairon maintained and practised a 'special relationship' with the police through direct contact with its organizational heads and even with officers in charge of the more important police stations. He used the intelligence wing of the police, under the charge of the Deputy Inspector-General (CID), to keep in detailed touch with the activities, both public and even personal, of the main political characters of the state. This information was used when necessary as an instrument of political power. In the public estimate, the liaison with the police carried the stigma of veiled conspiracy and even elements of the sinister. People complained that where political passions were involved, the officer in charge of a police station would not register as serious a crime such as murder without consultation with the chief minister, who often interested himself in the day-to-day investigation of cases.

Another activity which forged a close and intimate link with the police was Kairon's defined objective of 'rooting out corruption'. He wisely agreed to pursue this by strengthening institutional arrangements. He set up an Anti-Corruption (later renamed Vigilance) department under the charge of a whole-time civilian secretary and a separate police cell headed by a deputy inspector-general. Kairon was, however, so interested in the hunt for the corrupt that he would constantly refer particular events and officers for investigation on merest suspicion or complaint. The rumour got around that this might well include officials whom the chief minister, or his friends, did not like, and that the powers to order an investigation were used as a threat to ensure that independent action by an official was thwarted by fear of harassment resulting from police suspicion and enquiry. Thus the whole vigilance operation got enveloped in the fear that it was and could be used for a kind of blackmail.

It was inevitable that individual police officers, especially those dealing with intelligence in the districts, should be encouraged in these circumstances to enhance their importance, official recognition, and power by stepping over the line between what were personal activities of officials and their public impact. In one particular incident the CID reported that a set of officials were at a picnic at Pinjore, 'in which the party is alleged to have enjoyed drinking, meat and music'. The whole report was couched in terms implying excess and even immorality. Action against the participants for what was a rather harmless exercise of conviviality was avoided because the case happened to come to the chief secretary's notice and he was able to convince the chief minister of its essential triviality. Kairon's own ideas on this subject were clearly expressed, though difficult to translate into balanced practice:

Government servants are bound by rules and regulations in the conduct of
their official lives . . . It cannot, however, be said that they can or should be
allowed to go about their private-social life in any manner they like, particularly in the public eye, without there being anyone to point their lapses,
misdemeanour or misconduct . . . My idea is not to make the social-private life
of government servants more rigid or controlled, but to give it some semblance
of discipline where it comes into touch with or display in the public . . .

With the police not positively discouraged from stepping over the line,
and the chief minister avidly interested in information regarding
possible deviations in conduct, another element of fear was added to
the climate in which the administration worked.

Kairon faced and triumphed over two considerable political agitations launched by regional interests, the first by the *Hindu Raksha
Samiti* in 1957, which opposed the introduction of Punjabi in the
regional offices, and the second by the Akalis in 1960 in favour of a
Punjabi Suba. He was himself adamant against any further division of
the state and stood by the secular idea. He met regional pressures with
political skills and was always quick to concede any reasonable demand.
He took pains, for example, to concentrate on programmes for the
development of the comparatively backward hill region and for filling
institutional gaps in Haryana; he sought to meet the expressed fears of
the powerful Sikh minority. But when the parties endeavoured to gain
their point by agitation and courting arrest in the streets, he used the
full force of the police and insisted that the agitators should be appre-
hended and jailed in large numbers. Both agitations were broken and
called off. These strains, however, had the effect of enhanced importance
for the police and brought Kairon closer to them, particularly as
he insisted in conducting some of the operations personally, both
with reference to intelligence and even in the police control room
itself.

The cumulative influence of Kairon's dependence on, and use of the
police, was to create an atmosphere of suspicion and fear within the
civil administration and among political workers, especially those
opposed to Kairon and his men. In the Punjab the inspector-general of
the police was also *ex officio* a joint secretary to government, with the
power therefore to issue orders on its behalf. By convention this power
was only used in an emergency or to short-cut formalities. The fact that
it existed, however, lent support to the belief that even at headquarters
the police were not effectively under civil service control and might act
by direct contact with the political chief or, assuming his goodwill,
even on their own.

This put a strain on the delicate relationship between the district
officer and the superintendent of police to which reference has been
made in Chapter 2. The district magistrate felt increasingly that while

he was by definition in charge of law and order, in fact he was responsible but not in command. The superintendent, particularly where political nuances were involved, had a direct line of authority to headquarters and even the chief minister. Relations between the two wings of the district administration became at times tense. The problem was expressed, in terms of policy, by the demand of the civilian executive that the district magistrate should at least enjoy the definite power to record remarks in the annual confidential report on the superintendent of police. This was adamantly opposed by the police, from the inspector-general downwards. No redefinition of the subject took place and policy remained as in the British period. It now worked, however, with a degree of friction. The principle laid down in the constitution that judiciary and executive should be separated had gradually but progressively been worked into administrative arrangements in the Punjab. This also removed a source of strength that the district magistrate had enjoyed in relation to the police. As his authority over magistrates contracted, the police were not so dependent on his assistance and influence with them as they had been in the past.

Suspicion regarding Kairon's motives became a dominant trend in the Punjab and was soon extended to the appointments made during his regime to both the Public Service Commission and the High Court, though both these institutions are heavily protected by the constitution. This requires each state to have a Public Service Commission, appointed by the Governor (on the advice of his cabinet), each member assured a tenure from which he may not be removed except by resignation or procedure amounting to impeachment. The Commission was the state government's adviser on the recruitment of senior personnel and promotions of importance within the state services. Its advice might be ignored for valid recorded reasons, but whenever this was done the case had to be brought to the notice of the legislature, along with an annual report from the Commission itself. The legislature could thus ventilate, on the basis of independent information, any departures from accepted conventions of objective recruitment and promotion. The Commission's advice was almost invariably accepted and departure from it required decision by the cabinet.

The Commission was a brake on the government's freedom to hire and fire. Kairon was accused of attempting to 'pack' the Commission with persons amenable to his point of view or of a political background which would assist in the consolidation of his power. There is not adequate evidence categorically to support this criticism. The numbers in the Commission were certainly increased from three in 1956, when Kairon became chief minister, to four in 1957, and five in 1958. Kairon also selected during his eight years, as vacancies occurred, persons who had a political stake rather than an administrative past, and included personnel with a view to balancing regional pressures. He undoubtedly gave the selection and appointment of members a political significance, whereas previously they had been selected largely on an assessment of their competence by the chief recruiting agency of the state's services.

Procedure for appointments to the High Court of a state are even more stringent, requiring consultation in writing between the chief justice of the Court, the chief minister, and Governor of the state, and thereafter the home minister of the central government, the chief justice of the Supreme Court, and the Prime Minister. The appointment is formally made in the name of the President of India. Here again Kairon was suspected of 'fixing' a certain proportion of the appointments by prior informal consultation between himself, the chief justice, and the Governor. This accusation received some degree of confirmation from the fact that there was a substantial increase in the number of judges of the Court during 1956 to 1964 while he was chief minister. There were ten judges when he came to office, seventeen when he left. The number of appointments made in the period were sixteen, including vacancies by retirement and other causes. Against this interpretation is the fact that the number of cases instituted and pending in the High Court had grown enormously, following from the vast increase in laws and in procedural opportunities for redress by reference to courts, from the elaborate procedures of the Court itself, and from the faith of the public in recourse to judicial forums in preference to, and against the dictates of, executive decision.

A marked development in the Punjab, and in India, has been this enhanced public faith in the judiciary, whose prestige has risen out of all proportion and in significant contrast to a decline in that of the executive. Service conditions are also weighted in favour of the judiciary. Judges retire at the age of 62 in a High Court, 65 in the Supreme Court, as compared with 58 for the civil service; they are better paid and enjoy higher pensions. They are insulated from the direct firing line of meeting the public in the arena of executive circumstance and discretionary action. Yet the constitution does not prescribe an all-India service for the judiciary, in marked contrast to the British dispensation where a larger number of the district (and higher) judges came into their positions from the ICS. Now each state has a judicial service for appointments up to those of district judges. At that level and above persons are selected from the service and the bar. Most appointments to the High Court are from personnel who belong to the state. It is true that a High Court judge may be appointed from any part of India, as in final prescription it is an appointment by the President. The procedure and usage, however, in all but a minimal number of cases, restrict appointments to High Courts from the area served by each. High

Courts thus have an enormous bearing on the whole of the administrative situation but are selected on a narrower and more specialized basis
than the main executive administration.

Most of the strain of Kairon's methods fell on the general administrative services, particularly the IAS, which by 1956 had come to man
almost all the positions of district officers, most of those of non-
technical heads of departments, and several of the secretaries to government. The IAS made a good start and was well on its way to becoming,
as it was intended to be, the successor to the ICS. It was now limited
in numbers and in the state mostly confined to the higher supervisory
posts, and the 'supertime scale', above the rank of collector, while at
the Union level its members filled a variety of new assignments in
expanding administrative activities, including the economic field.

The IAS started with disadvantages. At independence the government decided to change the name from ICS to IAS, and to reduce the
emoluments. These decisions were primarily political, representing a
manifest and formal change from the colonial to the independent
regime. Over the years the gap in emoluments was made good, except
in pensions, by revisions of pay of particular posts and the creation of
new gradations of promotion. Nevertheless the name ICS had meant a
great deal in the leadership of the services and was well established with
the public. Discontinuing it was generally considered a setback by the
new service. This was now recruited 25 per cent by promotion of
officers of the state services, who came in at a more advanced age but
were permitted, in contrast to the British practice in regard to the then
15 per cent promoted officers, to take the name IAS on confirmation in
the service. The number of promoted officers usually exceeded 25 per
cent as they were physically available in the state; as government
expanded they immediately stepped into IAS positions, until a new set
of officers from the market could be recruited and trained. The politicians seemed to prefer the promoted officers to the younger direct
recruits as being more acquainted with the ways of the state and
possibly more pliable and amenable to local influence. Certainly Partap
Singh Kairon held this view. In discipline also the state civil service
officers were more intimately under the control of the local administration, whereas, once an officer formally entered the IAS, major disciplinary action against him could only be taken by the Union.

Apart from institutional arrangements, the needs of governments
following independence had led to a series of *ad hoc* recruitments to the
IAS, usually bringing in officers, from the market, at a higher spread of
ages than did open competition by examination, which restricted the
age of entry to between 21 and 24 years.

The integration of PEPSU with the Punjab at the end of 1956 led to
a giant operation of integrating all the services of that state with those

of the Punjab in common cadres. This work was performed by a series of committees, the highest in the state presided over by the chief minister, with a provision for appeals and policy guidelines to the Home Ministry of the Union. This process introduced yet another hetero- geneous element into the services generally, and had its influence also on the IAS. Some of the officers in the erstwhile princely states of PEPSU were of high calibre; many of them were not. They had found their way into government for reasons of family and friendship. Moreover the tradition of government in princely states had been largely, almost exclusively, personal. The key word in a prince's domain was *hookam* (order) and policy was frequently the ruler's *hookam*, right or wrong. The princes had little use for 'noting' in their decision-making!

Another consequence of the new system of mixed recruitment to the IAS was that officers had now got used to the idea, which was accepted by convention by the Government of India in practice, that direct recruits should step into the 'senior scale' (which meant the rank of collector or equivalent) after four years of work. One of the main reasons tending to make a defined period sacrosanct was the fact that the seniority of a promoted officer in the IAS took place from the date he started working in a senior scale post, so that if a directly recruited IAS officer did not get to the senior scale before him, he became his junior for the rest of his career. An insistence, therefore, on promotion to the senior scale at the end of four years had been generally recognized as a kind of right. In contrast, during the British period an officer did not enter the senior scale till there was a vacancy and he was judged to have the necessary experience for it; this was usually after six or even more years in the Punjab, though there had been periods following a shortage of officers when the senior scale was reached in three or four years.

The IAS had thus evolved by 1956 into a much more heterogeneous body of men than the ICS and was still in the process of being moulded into a top civil service, with a body of common administrative ex- perience, a strong sense of internal loyalty, and even stories and legends, shared between them. The youthfulness of the IAS had been somewhat tarnished, for though direct recruits achieved high responsibility at a young age, there were many others in the service who arrived at similar positions after promotion or *ad hoc* recruitment and who were already middle-aged.

In spite of these difficulties the IAS had settled in well in the Punjab and carried successfully and confidently the burden of administration thrown on them in consequence of the expansion of the government's interests and activities.

With the Kairon regime a new alignment of pressures and forces operated. The local boss, whether MLA or other political or social worker, now sought, and indeed took for granted, a direct line of communication with ministers. Kairon himself was the most accessible of men, and much of the local reputation of a politician or worker depended on whether, and how quickly, he could attract the government's concern at headquarters, and more especially that of the chief minister. The line between policy and implementation became thoroughly blurred. Often roles were ostensibly reversed. It was the local executive who was endeavouring to formulate general ideas to explain his action in particular cases to his clients in the district; whereas it was the secretariat that was pushing decisions on individual cases which had been thrust through the political line of communication, more particularly those in which the chief minister had expressed interest. In this medley of idea and action the terms and application of policy were not always clear, so that the official in the district often failed to obtain clear direction from his administrative superiors in the government, who were themselves not sure whether a particular decision would be supported by their political chiefs. Administration in a district implies a kind of contract between officer and public. He loses both initiative and confidence if the terms of that contract are not known, still more if they are not evenly applied. In such conditions the public also lose confidence and look for redress elsewhere. This situation gave considerable local discretion to the 'overmighty subjects' of the civil service, the men with a special relation with the chief minister who tended to believe and act as if they would be supported, on a plea of exigency, in whatever line they considered appropriate. The executive implementing agency was thus not adequately insulated from political interference in carrying out its tasks. There was an element of drama, and a battle of wits involved in keeping the administration in the districts running in order and with some degree of security to the mass of citizens.

It was not surprising that some officers, particularly the young, fell by the wayside. A direct recruit to the IAS might get his first district after four years, during which time he had worked in junior positions, and had not had the time or opportunity to become known to many of the civil servants at headquarters or to the ministers. There was thus no personal relation to protect and insulate him from the spate of complaints that might erupt on his first actions as a district officer. He was often overwhelmed and lost confidence at a stage of his career when this could do him permanent damage as an executive. After two or three cases of this kind, Kairon agreed that the policy should be to post direct IAS appointees for their first 'senior scale' responsibility to the secretariat, usually as deputy secretary, thus working under the guidance of a secretary, and providing also an opportunity for them to become known to both the senior officers and to some of the ministers before being sent out to the comparatively isolated responsibility of a district. This arrangement worked better. Kairon was essentially a kindly, generous man. Nevertheless his sense of mission and driving belief in his destiny as the agent of progress often compromised his manners and even the basic decencies in dealing with his officers.

To a certain extent elasticity about policy now became an instinctive, even deliberate, performance intended to provide for the exercise of patronage, which otherwise would have been dispensed by rule of thumb decisions by executive authority. This showed up especially in the administration of road transport, which had become a subject of economic importance and a source of valued patronage. The road system had grown tremendously since independence. In the Punjab, situated next to Delhi, a big consumer market, it was used on a large scale to carry services and goods; within the state also it was a crucial link with the railways for passengers and supplies. Further, state ownership was a subject of importance with Congress, especially after its declaration in 1954 for a 'socialistic pattern of society'. The Punjab had, in these circumstances, a mixed system; some transport routes, chiefly for passengers, were state-owned; the rest were controlled by 'route permits' provided to transporters. Profits were excellent; route permits were in great demand.

The main regulatory system was provided by law, but in its administration there was discretion which permitted a degree of manipulation. Thus the Regional Transport Authority, comprising the commissioner of a division of five to seven districts, with a statutory committee representing the various interests concerned including the railways and private transporters, decided how transport on the various routes should be regulated. There was provision for coordination, appeal and review by the State Transport Authority working under the orders of the minister for Transport.

The State Transport Authority was apt on occasion to suspend the authority of the Regional Transport Authority, ostensibly in order to examine particular situations and needs with a view to overall direction and regulation. The Commissioner of Ambala Division, chairman of the Regional Transport Authority, on one occasion refused to honour suspension by the State Transport Authority in regard to permits already decided on and announced. He held that these were valid in law and could only be set aside on the merits of particular cases after an appeal. The untidiness that resulted from this situation was settled by the passage of time rather than by clear definition or order. It withered away, but left an unpleasant trail of suspicions as to motives.

Another point of difficulty was in regard to who should hear appeals from the Regional Transport Authority's decisions. The civil service view was that this should be an officer senior to the commissioner who was chairman of the Regional Transport Authority. The political view, possibly somewhat inspired by the desire to retain elasticity in patronage, was that this should be the secretary of Transport, working under the minister. The fact that this officer was junior to the commissioner did not matter, as it was claimed that orders were passed on the authority of the government and not of the individual officer. The political view prevailed in the decision made by Kairon. The official assessment of this decision was that it was inspired by the wish to keep patronage within the political ambit.

The following incident reported by a private transporter was symptomatic of the way transport policy could be administered. This transporter, living in Delhi but operating on Punjab routes, said that for the 1962 general election he had been asked to supply two jeeps for use by the chief minister's political workers. The jeep is a highly useful vehicle for visits to villages over rough inter-connecting dirt roads. There is invariably a great demand, and an increase in the price, on the second-hand jeep market before an election. The transporter delivered the jeeps to the chief minister's men at Chandigarh. He received, no doubt in return though not defined as such, two temporary route permits, the earnings from which compensated him adequately. After the election he was told to call for the jeeps, and one was restored to him at Chandigarh. The second he learnt had been retained by a member of the Kairon family. Some weeks later he happened to meet Kairon, who expressed annoyance when he heard that the jeep had not been returned, and apparently took steps to see that it was. The transporter related this incident not in criticism but in praise of Kairon. He had need of the jeeps for the election, had ensured an adequate compensation for them in the temporary route permits, and had insisted on their return even though a member of his family had without his knowledge planned the contrary.

The public certainly believed that the transport trade was used as a crucial means of greasing the political machine, utilized at fever pitch especially near and during elections. The possible imposition, or extension, of nationalization also acted as a provocation to the trade to make the required concessions. It is likely that this situation was also exploited for private gain.

Partap Singh Kairon's drive for development necessarily put considerable emphasis on the technical services, especially the engineers in the three branches of the Public Works Department dealing with buildings and roads, electricity, and irrigation. He did not, however, subscribe to the view that the secretaries of technical departments should be technical men. He followed a mixed system when the choice lay with the government in particular situations. In this way the general manager of the Bhakra Dam, invariably an engineer, was also a secretary for his project; on the other hand the chief administrator of the Chandigarh capital was a 'generalist' and the secretary for the subject. The sharp friction between the generalists and specialists, which emerged in the later 1960s and reached confrontation in the 1970s was not a big problem at this time. Kairon was inclined in fact to use generalists for the position of secretary to government and appointed an ICS officer as secretary for Irrigation and Power in preference to an engineer. He also chose a generalist for secretary to the Education department.

Nor did Kairon interest himself in the proposition that headquarters should have a single unit of organization with the duties of secretary and head of department combined. He continued the British system of separation between the secretariat and the executive heads of a department, though his methods of work blurred the distinction between policy and implementation. One of Kairon's political compromises threw some indirect light on the value of a two-tier organization. In 1956 he agreed, as a result of Sikh regional pressure, that all cases where the government had passed disciplinary orders against officials should be reviewed by a special agency. It was decided that the cabinet would accept the Governor's orders given in his personal judgement, that is without advice of the minister. The object of this was to satisfy Sikh opinion that officials of their community had not been discriminated against by the Hindu majority, though the review of the cases did not confine itself to this particular point but extended to the merits of the orders passed. I was given the task of examining these cases and preparing briefs for the Governor's orders. Of 231 cases examined, orders were reversed only in 34, and modified partially in 31. There was no evidence of communal (religious) bias in the decisions; in fact, minorities seemed to be treated with considerable care. There was, however, distinct evidence that cases were examined with greater care, and more meticulous detail, where there were two tiers of authority at headquarters. Possibly the existence of two units examining the same material ensured more balanced and comprehensive assessment.

Kairon's headlong thrust for action at all levels of government and in direct dealings with both officials and the public, often ignoring the lines of command, kept the Secretariat fully occupied in clearing the debris and fulfilling the requirements of law and rule, as well as in maintaining morale and corporate effort in the services. This task was performed at an adequate level to ensure many-sided development and progress, which achieved for the Punjab the position it still commands, as the state with the highest per capita income in India and as a primary wheat producer with yields comparable to the best in the world.

But neither Partap Singh Kairon, nor the administration, was able to save him from the suspicion, hate, and fury that his methods provoked.

The demands for an enquiry into his conduct, particularly the allegations that his sons made business and money through his power and
influence, grew to an extent where a Commission of Inquiry was
appointed by Nehru at the end of 1963, as a means of assuaging and
satisfying his opponents. Kairon readily agreed and undertook to
resign if he was held guilty on any count. The Commission, comprising
a single judge, the retired Chief Justice S. R. Das of the Supreme Court,
exonerated him on most of the charges formulated by his political
opponents but declared that on some allegations he had, with knowledge, allowed his power and influence to be used to help his sons. The
Commission reported on 11 June 1964 and Kairon stepped down from
office and power on the 24th. He quit with dignity and carried himself
with self-respect thereafter as a loyal Congress MLA.

As far as can be analysed, it was not any opposing principle, or even
provoked vested interests, that removed Kairon from power. Nor did
the system of administration offer any resistance that could have forced
Kairon to drive it to a state of disrepair and intense suspicion of his
motives. This very administrative system had during the war decided
important cases, from clerk to Governor, through the serried ranks of
hierarchy, often in a single day. Its capacity to act quickly and effectively
depended on a build-up of comprehension regarding intentions and
priorities. That build-up, which created almost a conspiracy to govern,
had perhaps been, understandably and naturally, impaired by the many
voices of new democracy expressed in the universal vote, and the vast
increase in the area of governance. That build-up could have been
achieved again but the means, in a democracy, would have to be
educative and moral, not abrasive and authoritarian. Kairon obviously
failed to see this. In a short time, he laid a foundation for deep suspicion
and distrust, which his enemies used to create a volume of corruption
and nepotism enough to sweep him from power.

Fate decreed a yet more dramatic end for him. On 6 February 1965
he was forced out of his car, in broad daylight, and shot dead on the
Grand Trunk Road, twenty miles from Delhi.

Even two decades after his resignation, he remains a controversial
figure in regard to his impact on administration and politics. There is
agreement that he awakened the state and stirred it to a tremendous
effort in self-reliant development. That he brought the whole administrative system to a degree of contempt with the people and of
disarray within itself, is true also. He himself had a contempt for and
impatience with it. He relied extensively on information that did not
come from responsible cadres. This encouraged the erosion of morale
and reduced discipline. It did not nurture a feeling of security or justice,
only fear and hostility to personal rule.

There are many who believe that Kairon's methods had a deep and adverse influence on public conduct throughout India, that he set in motion methods of manipulation, the use of power and money to buy friends and beat opponents, blackmail and intimidation of both politicians and administrators. These methods have, it is alleged, flourished more widely following his example.

It is unlikely that Kairon had any influence on the public life of India as a whole; there is no doubt that, in the Punjab, he brought the politics of the bazaar and the village into the daily business of administration. But the forces thus released have not even now sorted themselves out in orderly relationships of mutual interplay or comprehended responsibility. These forces were not contained. Kairon's impact on administration in the Punjab was an indication of its strength and its weakness. It was strong in being able and willing to respond to dynamic political direction. It delivered the services required of it. It was weak in that it did not apparently preserve that minimum core of administrative decisions and services that would assure a sense of security and justice to its citizens. The whole atmosphere became charged with suspicion, resentment, and hate. Public opinion organized and made Kairon the symbol of its hate, wrenching power from him, not by process of election, but by the extraordinary sanction of a special investigation.

The history of the Punjab, following Kairon's fall from power and his murder, both crucified him further and vindicated him. In 1966, the Union government conceded *Punjabi Suba*, which Kairon had so staunchly opposed. The Punjab was further divided into two states, Punjab (1971 population, 13.55 million) and Haryana (10.04 million), with three districts handed over to the hill state of Himachal Pradesh. On the other hand, in the years following Kairon's demise, both Punjab and Haryana garnered and consolidated their tremendous increase in agricultural production, the main though by no means the only economic advance in this part of India. Politically the scene has been unsettled and difficult. The Punjab has not thus far thrown up a leadership that offers any prospect of confidence or durability. Disillusionment also set in following the 'triumph' of the *suba*. Many Punjabis refer to the *suba* as *subi* (diminutive, used in a derogatory sense). Many speak with nostalgia of Kairon.

8

JAMMU AND KASHMIR STATE, 1964–1967

In the bitter cold of early January 1964, when freezing winds blew from the snowpeaks that surround the valley and the sun scarcely penetrated for the few hours that it was in the sky, Srinagar, the capital city of Jammu and Kashmir, was in the grip of the rule of its crowds, whose whims were law. They came out, despite the frozen snow in the streets, in their thousands, including women, often bent in the unison of prayer in the Islamic tradition, round the squares, particularly the Lal Chowk. Their leaders controlled the movement of traffic and of persons, including the officers of the law. Black for mourning was the order of the day. Even the transport of the powerful and feared deputy inspector-general of police was required to fly a black flag and could only ply with permission. The small minority Hindu community, in Srinagar described collectively as 'Kashmiri Pandits', joined the Muslim majority in mourning. The crowd took scrupulous care to ensure that no member of the minority religion should be molested or threatened in any way, and belied the fear that the tension would break out into religious riot and arson.

The cause of this universal demonstration was the theft of the *Mua Muquadas*. This was a strand of hair believed to originate from the Prophet of Islam, which tradition, including a long legend of bloody and intricate incident, insisted was kept at the Hazratbal Mosque in Srinagar. It was in the charge of the priests and on special occasions, usually the big Islamic festivals, *deedhar* (a view) of the *Mua Muquadas* was permitted to those gathered for worship. The holy hair, which could not be moved from its place in the mosque and in spite of strict observances for its safety, had disappeared. The city of Srinagar was plunged into mourning and protest against the government during whose regime this sacrilege had been perpetrated. The *Mua Muquadas* was quite as dramatically replaced and restored to the custody of the priests. Order returned to the city and tension disappeared as suddenly as it had arrived.

What had happened? One story puts the blame on Pakistan, ever on the watch for stirring up trouble, especially with any religious implications, in the valley. But if so, why was the holy hair returned? Was the thief afflicted by the unbearable burden of sudden remorse, or some dire manifestation from God? Another story believes that the powerful

Prime Minister of the state, Bakshi Ghulam Mohammad, had used his influence with the priests to borrow the hair in order to give solace to his ailing mother. He restored it as surreptitiously when he saw the upsurge of mass feelings its absence had created. The truth may possibly never emerge. The holy hair was back but Bakshi Ghulam Mohammad was swept from power and did not regain it. He died in 1972.

Bakshi Ghulam Mohammad had been Prime Minister of the state since 1953 and exercised dominating, almost exclusive, power until 1964. He had come up from the rank and file of transport workers to become one of the leading politicians in the National Conference, the political party founded in 1933 that stood for responsible government and independence. In fact the aims of the party were similar to those of the Indian National Congress, but as the Maharaja of Kashmir, who had ruled this princely state, had banned both Congress and Jinnah's Muslim League it operated under the name of National Conference and was a separate entity.

At the time of the 1947 invasion of Kashmir this party, led by Sheikh Abdullah, had two deputies in the line of command, Bakshi Ghulam Mohammad and Ghulam Mohammad Sadiq, of whom the latter was considered the more mature and senior, but Bakshi had more drama and the greater flair for public relations. He was able, on Abdullah's arrest in 1953, to step into his place as Prime Minister.

Bakshi was a man of diverse and incessant action, of many and varied associates. He rewarded service and loyalty at all levels with recognition and friendship. However he established one-man rule in the state and reduced his colleagues in the cabinet to yesmen or drove them to opposition. Among the latter, Sadiq opposed Bakshi, at first in the council, and later outside it, taking with him two political stalwarts, Mir Qasim, the chief minister of Kashmir today, and D. P. Dhar, now the planning minister for India.

Bakshi's methods and means of maintaining power were similar to Kairon's. The differences between the two were that Bakshi was primarily a townsman, and such development work as he did was confined to the urban areas; the villages remained substantially untouched; Bakshi also took great pains to preserve good relations with his officials. But like Kairon he acquired the reputation of depending heavily on the police, of being unscrupulous in dealing with opposition, and assisting his relations and friends to influence and money. He had become the object of grave all-round suspicion to many, and even hate to some.

The *Mua Muquadas* incident brought the forces against him to a head. He was for some days unable even to appear in public and the only violence indulged in by the crowd was against the property of his relations and friends. It was evident that he would have to step down from power. For a few weeks, following the events of early January 1964, a *via media* was attempted by selecting one of Bakshi's 'yesmen' as Prime Minister, from which came the expression, now used in North India, 'doing the Shamsuddin' in politics, meaning putting in a figurehead as the ostensible boss while the power lay elsewhere. But the mood of the people, and the strength that Sadiq had built up over the years, made short work of this compromise. He was elected leader at the end of February 1964, and continued as such until his death in 1972. I worked as his chief secretary from March 1964 to the middle of 1967, on loan to his state from the Punjab under arrangements made by the Union.

Administration in this state is more than usually influenced by the character of the land and the culture of its people. It is in many ways a museum—in the first place one of terrains. The entry into the Indian part of Jammu and Kashmir, as held by the cease-fire line of 1949, is from the railhead at Pathankot (extended to Jammu in 1972). The river Ravi is crossed ten miles from Pathankot to enter the state. Fifty-seven miles of low-lying, undulating land, cut up by stony, infertile soil, with the beds of many seasonal streams that become torrents during the rains, mark the way to Jammu, the winter capital. From Jammu, up hills and down to the depths of several valleys, the road rises to 7,000 feet at Patnitop, down again to 2,000 feet at Ramban where the river Chenab is crossed, and on to the Nehru Tunnel at over 7,000 feet, in all 120 miles from Jammu. The country up to the tunnel, where the Jammu administrative region ends, is interspersed on both right and left with tremendous valleys and high hills, with habitations nestling among them at heights varying from 2,000 to 10,000 feet. One diversion to the west and north of Jammu runs through the Poonch-Rajouri area, bordering the cease-fire line and Pakistan-occupied Kashmir.

The heart of the state, however, in legend, beauty, and history, is the valley of Kashmir, beyond the Banihal Pass. This pass is over 9,000 feet high but the Nehru Tunnel below attempts to ensure an all-weather road into the valley, which lies below and beyond it, at a height of 5,000 feet, the largest inhabited expanse of almost flat land at this elevation. The valley is surrounded by some of the loftiest mountains of the world, to the north and west by peaks rising to well over 20,000 feet, many of them continuously covered in snow, several still unvisited by man, and others visited only by intrepid itinerant shepherds, who in the summer bring their sheep to graze on the nourishing pastures at these heights. At the head of the valley, just below Banihal where the plain starts, is Verinag, the source of the river Jhelum, a group of perennial springs.

The Jhelum river falls but a few feet, meandering lazily through the vast plain of the valley, through Anantnag, the valley's second city, to Baramulla, its third, eighty miles away. The river is used for navigation and for the irrigation of paddy fields, which produce some of the highest yields of rice in India. It is also a home for many people who live in house-boats tethered to its banks, and among the many inlets and lakes that the bed of the river forms. The largest of these lakes is the Dal at Srinagar, which attracts thousands of tourists in the summer. The Nagin Lake, also at Srinagar, more idyllic in seclusion and beauty, was built by Shah Jehan. Around and along the Dal the Mughal emperors and their counsellors laid a series of gardens on ascending levels, in the traditional Islamic style. Hence the Chashma Shahi (the King's Spring), the Shalimar (after which 'pale hands I love beside the Shalimar') and the Nishat. Much of the beauty and splendour of the valley lies in the combination it enjoys of flat plain, towering mountains, and an abundance of water.

The state proceeds beyond the valley, over the Zogila Pass, to the plateau of Ladakh at 10,000 to 13,000 feet, with the capital town of the district at Leh, 12,000 feet, one of the highest habitations in the world. The plateau is above the tree line and the hills here have much of the appearance of desert, but massively uneven, as if the gods in unison had haphazardly flung down great mounds of giant rock. Little grows except with great effort; water is brought, often from the heights of snowfed sources, by canals chiselled out of the sheer rock. Beyond Leh are miles of inaccessible hills with here and there hazardous foot-paths and, beyond that, the borders of the People's Republic of China.

Matched with its terrain, the state is also a museum of flora and fauna. The valley is affluent, indeed bursting, with many varieties of flower and fruit. Its apples, cherries, apricots, plums, and walnuts are famed far beyond the state, but owing to difficulties of movement and preservation do not bring the return they should to the people. At Pampore, near Srinagar, is one of the few areas of the world where saffron flourishes. The valley is the only home in India of the magnificent Chinar tree, originally an import from Persia, but surpassing its parent in splendour.

The Government of India's compilation of information states: 'Principal languages: Kashmiri, Ladakhi, Dogri, Balti, Dardi and Pahari. Official language: Urdu'. That is only part of the story; dialects vary almost from valley to valley and ridge to ridge. The state today, of India's twenty-one, is the sixth largest in area (222,000 square kilometres) and the sixth smallest in population (4.6 million). By religion it has, according to the 1971 census:

Muslims	3,040,000
Hindus	1,404,000
Christians	7,000
Sikhs	105,000
Buddhists	58,000
Jainis	1,000
Others	negligible

Most of the Muslim population is concentrated in the valley with some below the Banihal Ridge but nearer the valley (in the districts of Doda, Poonch and Rajouri). The Hindus are mostly in the middle and lower Jammu region, and the Buddhists almost exclusively in Ladakh, where they are more than half the population, the remainder being mostly Muslim.

While there are marginal overlaps, the population of the valley, both Muslim and non-Muslim, are Kashmiri-speaking and of that culture, while the population below the passes are non-Kashmiri in tradition and language. This is particularly true of the vast bulk of the Muslim population of the districts of Poonch and Rajouri, who are popularly known as 'Poonchis' and speaking a language of that name which carries strong traces of Punjabi and Pahari. The Poonchis have a strong military tradition and, unlike the Kashmiris, for decades have sought service in the armed forces. This position was no doubt assisted by policy as the Maharaja-Dogra rule used the Poonchis and Dogras for their military and police services. The Kashmiris, however, tend to be insular, and there is practically no intermarriage between them and persons from outside the valley. They regard an excursion even to Jammu, for any length of time, as a deprivation. The Kashmiri pandits (Hindus) are to some extent an exception; no doubt originally goaded by waves of religious persecution going back far into Kashmir's history of the pre-British period, they have for generations migrated to the plains where many families, including the Nehrus, settled to find permanent homes.

Another unusual feature of the valley is that among the Hindus there is practically only one caste, the Brahmins. This again is connected with periods of religious persecution, when most of the other Hindus were forcibly converted to Islam and only a few were clever enough or useful enough to be able to remain as Hindus. The result is that the valley has never in living memory witnessed the practices and the rigidities of the caste system.

While there are practically no Buddhists in the valley today, signs of this common heritage from the past survive and perhaps explain many attitudes in this society. It is difficult to distinguish a Muslim mosque from a Hindu temple; both are built in the same style, with marked features of the Buddist *vihara*. Many occasions and locations are held in esteem by both Hindus and Muslims, even supported jointly. Even today every local bus or taxi driver will slow down at Anantpur, twenty miles from Srinagar, to drop a few coins outside the mosque there, famed for centuries for its care of travellers. At the Hindu temple of Baba Rishi both communities visit and offer alms, by tradition invariably in kind, to propitiate the divinity to obtain a child for the family, particularly a son. The cave of Amar Nath is the object of an annual pilgrimage by thousands of Hindus from all over India. It is a walk each way of some fifty-four miles from Pahalgam, over a pass of 15,000 feet, to the cave itself at 12,000. The last lap lies over a snow-bridge, across the bed of an avalanche, where the only signs of life are the occasional marmosets, warm-looking and snug in their thick furs, peeping suddenly from holes in the snow. As a token of humility, some of the faithful perform the pilgrimage by measuring their body, length after length, on the ground to cover the distance to the cave, where the ice is supposed to form in the shape of a 'lingam' hanging from its roof. This cave and its environs venerated for generations by Hindus, is owned by a Muslim family of Maliks.

Nor are the religions in the valley divided by dietary habits. Both Muslims and Hindus, when they can afford it, love eating meat. As affluence increases, the number and variety of meat dishes increase. Where incomes permit both communities drink alcohol. This is in marked contrast to the plains of India where Hindu society has been generally vegetarian and Muslim society has regarded alcohol as taboo.

Both Muslim and Hindu families often carry the same surname, for example Multo, Karr, Dar, Kitchloo, and a host of others. Even Pandit may be a Muslim surname, though in the rest of India associated almost exclusively with the Brahmin caste.

The fact is that the culture of the valley cuts across religion. Kashmiris share a way of life including a common tradition of language, drama, and song, above all a common historic experience and memory. Citizens of both religions have been subjected to grim devastation at the hands of outside invaders and exploiters. Most of these were Muslims, particularly the cruel Pathans. Life and women were held in scant respect by the invaders; forcible conversion was merely an added hobby. An exception to this were the Mughals who, once they had established themselves, behaved like affluent and good-humoured tourists. The non-Muslim occupation was that of the Sikhs and Dogras, and while this was by no means benevolent or popular, it was not positively vicious. Yet even this has left a scar and the Kashmiri generally shares a suspicion of the people, including Muslims, from the Punjab.

These circumstances may also explain the fact that the Kashmir valley and Ladakh have never been the scene of the kind of rabid 'communalism' (religious tension and hate) that has often marred the relations of the religions—Hindu and Muslim—in the plains of India, unless such communalism and persecution has been imported into the valley. A marked example of this was in 1947-48, when in the Jammu region of the state, the Muslim minority suffered a violent attack and the Hindus on the Pakistan side were driven out altogether. In spite of the grave provocation, there were no reprisals in the valley, where the Hindu minority, less than four per cent, could have been wiped out. Gandhi proclaimed that Kashmir was an example to India. Apart from minor aberrations, usually inspired, paid for, and organized by outside influence, the people of the valley have preserved, and in crisis defended, the highest standards of tolerance.

In the state the tradition of administration was highly centralized and personal, even in 1964. While the facade was now similar to that of the Punjab, the services depended greatly on initiative, expressed or covert, from the top. This was partly an inheritance from princely Maharaja rule, which had continued from Sikh times through the British period. Many of the officers of the civil administration had been recruited to it by the Maharaja from among the influential families loyal to the ruler. Their standard of education was usually good, but there was the tradition of *ashaira* (meaning indication or gesture), that is, performance following the personal priorities of the court, particularly the Maharaja's. If he was keen on schools there would be schools; if he was keen on palaces, there would be palaces.

On its integration with India, in the special circumstances of the invasion of its territory with the support of Pakistan, the state drew up a constitution for itself, and for all practical purposes established the institutions of a state of the Union and responsible government. Effective power was indeed wrested from the Maharaja and transferred to elected representatives of the people.

It was the character and personalities of the first two popular Prime Ministers and the critical relations with Pakistan that had so far moulded the climate of the administration. Both Sheikh Mohammad Abdullah (1947-53) and Bakshi Ghulam Mohammad were strong, self-willed personalities. They continued a highly personalized administration where the drive lay with them and a few chosen individuals. This fitted in with the kind of government people had known and did not meet with surprise or resistance. Much of Bakshi's business was transacted at a Sunday morning gathering at his house; no one was specially invited but everyone who was anyone in the crucial decision-making process was present. If you did not, or could not, secure entry, you did not in fact partake in these decisions.

This continuation, for a prolonged period, of centralized, almost personal, government no doubt owed its survival to the presence of Pakistan as an untiring contestant for jurisdiction in Kashmir. The problem was kept alive in all the forums of international politics and by activity through agents in the state. Pakistan endeavoured to build her image as the saviour of the Book and the Prophet, the protector of Islam, and the natural heir to a Muslim majority area contiguous to her boundaries.

Ghulam Mohammad Sadiq became Prime Minister in February 1964 determined to achieve a more decentralized administrative and political life. 'Normalization', 'liberalization', and 'politicalization' were three words that he often employed to define his aims, apart from development programmes that previous governments had also sought. In this he was in fact endeavouring to bring about a revolution, for custom and usage had thus far charted a different part.

The government's 'Rules of Business' meant that a great amount of trivia went to the cabinet. Even the sanction of a clerk's post required their approval. *Prima facie* the solution was a simple matter of working out adequate delegation; in fact it was not so, as the habit of mind and the tradition of balance in the use of delegated powers had not developed. When delegation took place it tended to be used as a ready, now legal, means of exercising personal or political patronage, or regarded as a trust so awful to use that paralysis followed.

The salaries of executives were small, except for a few officers of the all-India services, who enjoyed the prescribed emoluments of their cadres. A local collector or head of department usually had a pay-scale about half of that in other parts of India. An IAS officer would receive Rs 1,000 to 1,850 a month, a local official 500 to 1,000; and so on, all along the line. This was part of the Maharaja tradition, where emoluments were often made good by recognized favours, a grant of land, the cost of educating a son, even a wardrobe of clothing for a ceremonial occasion. There was also a tradition of living off the land and the environment. This had been part of accepted convention and perhaps for that reason practised within moderate and decent terms.

The secretariat kept the briefest record of the pros and cons of policy. Many cabinet decisions were not preceded by memoranda but merely records of a decision taken, often on a problem verbally presented by a minister. Many appointments and promotions were made with no means of establishing why A had been preferred to B. Several officers of government had been in politics and vice versa. D. P. Dhar, the home minister in 1964, had previously been home secretary; Mir Qasim, the number two politician to Sadiq, had been the personal assistant to a previous revenue minister. Records of age were controversial, and as officers approached retirement claims were made that they were younger than they really were.

Though administration had functioned in this way, much of it had been dispensed with humane and kindly instinct. The Kashmiri believes in and has a feel for compromise. He will argue with the greatest show of violence. The nearer he gets to the object of his abuse the gentler are his manifestations of wrath; the deal is often clinched with an affectionate embrace. Yet there had been a distinct public feeling that Bakshi had over-stepped the line in his use of the police and abuse of patronage.

Sadiq thus had much to change. He wished to organize a system where responsibility and initiative would be dispersed to smaller, lower units of action, and yet made effective. He was a slow-moving man, more sound and thoughtful than dramatic, but persevering. His was an educated temperament, with many of the qualities of a university don rather than a politician in a state under fire. He delegated much of the touring, visiting, and speaking to his political lieutenants. He was firm in bringing the state back to normal, stabilized conditions. He put through important changes at the political level. He persuaded the Union government to release Sheikh Abdullah, and met the consequences of this in subdued, but precise, application of the law. Executives were told that they would receive no support from government if there was valid criticism and abuse against their actions, but they must take immediate action against even the possibility of violence. He modified the constitution so that the state in future had a Governor, not the special 'Sadr-i-Riyasat'. He changed the designation of 'Prime Minister' to 'Chief Minister', and merged the National Conference into a state branch of the Indian National Congress.

In administration, powers were defined and delegated to ministers and departments; the state started accepting, for the first time, a regular quota of IAS and Indian Police Service officers. A state civil service was organized with provision for future recruitment primarily by open, advertised competitive selection. To meet public clamour against the Bakshi regime, a commission of inquiry, with a judge from outside the state, was established to report on the allegations against him.

Sadiq had touching faith in the arts and in education. He retained these subjects for long in his own portfolio, in spite of pressure that the chief minister should not be too involved in gardens—of considerable importance in a tourist dependent area—sculpture, history, and aesthetics.

It is difficult to assess how far, and how fast, Sadiq would have gone. Plans and programmes of ordinary, even 'pedestrian' development, so dear to his heart, were swept aside by the Pakistan invasion of 1965.

Manifestations of the running sore of the Pakistan problem in the state had been a constant, almost daily, problem for the administration. Pakistan's object was to keep the 'Kashmir issue' alive in the diplomatic shop window, and an important means to this end was the creation of an impression, and preferably also the actual fact, of seething unrest in the state. Different programmes of action to these ends were planned for the predominantly Hindu Jammu region, the Muslim Poonch-Rajouri area to the northwest of that region, and the Kashmir valley itself.

In the Jammu Hindu area a state of constant unrest was maintained all along the cease-fire line. There were raids into villages at the border, accompanied by cattle-stealing, arson, and murder. There were incidents of sabotage even in the interior. A bomb exploded in 1964 in a cinema in Jammu itself, killing a student and injuring others; another burst near the assembly building in the heart of the town. It would be incorrect to assume that all the activity was initiated by Pakistan. In any event, an eye for an eye and a tooth for a tooth, better still two of each, was often found by India to be the most effective deterrent in curbing Pakistan. Redress against violence was sought in violence. The fact is that for Pakistan it was positive policy to create and keep unrest alive; for India it was certainly positive policy to prevent, and apply remedies to cure, these eruptions. The Jammu cease-fire line was indeed a 'live' border, bristling with tension and the scene of destruction of property and murder of innocent civilians.

In the Poonch-Rajouri area the population was predominantly Muslim. Here there was kinship of language and culture as well as religion between persons on both sides of the Indo-Pakistan cease-fire line border. There was even intermarriage between villages. The terrain was broken up by hills and valleys, at altitudes mostly between 2,000 and 5,000 feet, though some of the hills were even higher. Entry all along the cease-fire line could not be watched. There was considerable coming and going. Contacts were maintained and built up. In times of formal peace there was no organized campaign of violence, arson, or looting. Many of the exchanges between the populations were in fact ignored by both sides.

It was in the Kashmir valley that the biggest prize lay. Here also the terrain was susceptible to surreptitious entry, but the hills and valleys were higher and deeper in isolation. Except for a few families on the immediate border, there was a cultural and language barrier with the Pakistanis. These were Kashmiri-speaking Indians; there was little intermarriage; the communication and supply lines were easier from the towns of the valley, particularly Srinagar and Baramulla, than from Pakistan-occupied Kashmir. The people knew and had contact with a government in the valley, headed by a popularly elected chief minister and officials responsible to him, whereas Pakistan-occupied Kashmir was manifestly controlled by the army. In spite of these disadvantages Pakistan maintained contact through its paid agents. These were concentrated mostly in the towns of the valley—Srinagar, Anantnag, and Baramulla—and operated through the mosques. The *mullas* (priests) and *maulvis* (religious teachers) were in the vanguard of the movement. Religion provided the rallying platform. Pakistani activity was directed at seizing every opportunity to heighten and create religious tension and cleavage. Propaganda and action was particularly directed to discrediting the Indian army, as infidels holding the countryside against its will, and an instrument of suppression and subjugation. The local government were described as puppets of the army. The campaign was supported by constant programmes on the radio, in both Urdu and Kashmiri. Whatever its influence in Jammu and Kashmir, Pakistan propaganda certainly succeeded in giving its government a bad reputation for corruption and ill-will abroad.

Pakistan also devoted, through its agents, considerable attention to the United Nations Military Observer Group (UNMOG) based partly at Srinagar and partly in Rawalpindi (in Pakistan). They were constantly petitioned at Srinagar with allegations regarding the suppression of civil liberties and enormities committed by the administration and army.

Suddenly, on 5 August 1965, it was discovered that Pakistan had infiltrated, with groups of armed personnel, to vantage points behind the border, some of them within a few miles of Srinagar, as well as in the Poonch-Rajouri area and along the long road leading to Kargil and Leh. These were small detachments of fifty to two hundred men, operating with great mobility, well supplied with arms and Indian currency, and in communication with their base in Pakistan-occupied Kashmir and Pakistan. Some thousands entered the state. Their method of operation was to move into a village, where they sought shelter, food, and guides, for which, at the start of operations, they had money to pay, and then to attack vantage points wherever they found these inadequately protected. They avoided a fight and usually attacked only by massacring any forces obviously inferior. Many policemen were killed, some police stations captured. Targets of repeated attack were bridges all along the long road through the hills, the crucial supply line to the valley and Ladakh.

A war against infiltrators is by no means solely a military operation. The civilian administration, particularly the police, and the public were immediately and heavily involved. The infiltrators received little support or comfort from the villages in the valley and failed in the main objects of their initiative, which were apparently to disrupt the supply route, and to capture some positions, like public offices and radio stations, as bases for causing disarray among the civilian population and paralysis in the administration. They certainly inflicted death and a degree of devastation. These included the burning down of Batamaloo, a suburb of Srinagar, a residential area of some two hundred and fifty houses. On the whole, however, except in the Poonch-Rajouri area, their whole effort proved abortive and futile. Once the Indian army opened attack, in defence of the state, on the Pakistan fronts towards Sialkot and Lahore, on 5 September 1965, the infiltrators were finally swept from the valley in a matter of hours, and from the state in days. The invasion ended finally with the cease-fire with Pakistan on 23 September and the Tashkent agreement of January 1966.

The organization of resistance to the infiltration was a task of considerable dimensions, particularly in coordination between army, police, and public. Intelligence from villages was of crucial importance in the hill terrain, to spot centres of trouble and to ensure assistance to attack these without the foreknowledge of the enemy. This was put through, primarily under overall army direction, effectively and quickly, to the discomfort and speedy rout of the infiltrators.

The state, however, received a considerable setback to Sadiq's pursuit of normalcy. In the Poonch-Rajouri area the infiltrators had succeeded in polarizing the major religions, with the result that a large number of the minority Hindu population moved out into refugee camps along the main road. Another group of refugees had moved out of the Chhamb area in the southwest where fierce fighting between the armed forces took place. Considerable effort had to be directed to resettling these persons, just under 100,000 in number. There had been much damage to housing in both areas.

In spite of this setback the state was back to fairly normal conditions by the summer of 1966, when a record tourist season for the valley seemed to usher in a turn from the misfortunes of war. Sadiq was re-elected chief minister with a strong majority in 1967, and the state appeared to be more stable and normal than it had been since 1947.

In Appendix II I give some observations on certain aspects of the Kashmir problem.

In 1967 I had completed eight years of work as chief secretary in two states and it is appropriate to underline changes that had taken place in this position after independence. The chief secretary, already of significant influence in 1947 as the point where coordination of policy was centred, became even more important in a political regime with a cabinet heading the government. Here was the apex and the hub, the point where politicians and administrators met to work out the patterns for the formulation of policy and the methods for implementing programmes. The chief secretary was in many ways the interpreter who conveyed the limits, and often the difficulties, of the civil service to the political chiefs in regard to alternative policies, and in turn took to the services the political requirements as defined by the leadership. This was not merely, however, a matter of communication but at its best also the building up of morale, understanding, and sympathy, so essential to constructive, smooth implementation of policy. Bhim Sen Sachar indeed described the main function of the chief secretary as that of 'the chief minister's conscience'. This process was continuous, emerging over a series of cases, many of them individual, others of a general nature, which went to the chief minister and even to cabinet.

The development of this enhanced, indeed unique, importance of the chief secretary was a reversal of the carefully nurtured practice of the British Raj, where the symbol of its highest priority was the branch of government headed in the Punjab by the financial commissioner, which dealt with the bulk of citizens in the land revenue agency.

In 1964 Partap Singh Kairon appointed one of the financial commissioners as his chief secretary, allowing him to continue with the higher pay of the former post. This was a distinct departure from previous practice according to which the chief secretary would be promoted to financial commissioner at an appropriate time. It was, however, an indication of a change in the respective esteem now given to the two positions.

Similar developments must have been taking place elsewhere in the country. In 1970 the Union government, in consultation with the states, raised the pay of the chief secretary—for those states which approved it which were the vast majority—to that of a secretary to the Government of India. This change has carried the process even further than Kairon did. The chief secretary is now the sole position at state level which carries the highest civil service pay in India. One of the reasons given for this change was that it would enable the most senior officers of the service to return from Delhi to work in the states.

The results of these developments in relation to the position and utility of the chief secretary have apparently been adverse. State governments are now faced with difficulties on almost every appointment. If they do not appoint the most senior officer in the state they are involved in supersession and discontent; if they do, their choice is greatly limited for a position that, for proper performance, requires not merely experience but imagination and humanity in evolving relations between civil servants and ministers. To meet this situation several untidy expedients have been adopted. One is to give the financial commissioner the same salary as the chief secretary when the most senior man is not selected. This is expensive and hardly avoids resentment. Another has been to send the most senior officer to the Union government, sometimes even against his wishes or alternatively to get an officer back from the Union.

This situation has also created the opportunity for some to allege ulterior motives for selection and for officers to endeavour at times to manoeuvre themselves into favourable postures in advance of selection. The appointment has thus become involved with politics, or at least given rise to the strong suspicion that it is; this reduces the influence of the chief secretary with the services and thus causes the position to lose much of its value to the government. In the Punjab from 1968 to 1973 there have been as many as four chief secretaries, some of whom have been ejected on a change of government without ceremony or grace.

Yet another expedient is to reduce the practical importance of the position by transferring effective decision-making to another officer. This has happened most significantly in Haryana where decision-making advice, particularly about personnel, rests with the chief minister's secretary. There is then a cleavage between *de facto* and *de jure* influence within the administration, which brings its own problems. In such circumstances the chief secretary is broadly reduced to keeping straight the records of decisions and actions in his sphere, which are in fact taken elsewhere. It also creates the impression, among both services and public, of a personalized regime run by the chief minister. The secretariat in this event weakens its essential service to the government of being a repository of information, experience, and judgement, available to ministers for their determination of policy and their supervision of action, and submitted to them fully, frankly, and responsibly both in writing and in discussion.

9

THE MINISTRY OF PETROLEUM AND CHEMICALS, 1967–1971

The Union secretariat, and the headquarters offices of the central government had long before 1967 expanded far beyond the accommodation that Lutyens' New Delhi had provided or even envisaged. In that year the decision was made that the secretariat, comprising the imposing red sandstone structures of the North and South Blocks, was adequate only for the four ministries of Home, External Affairs, Defence, and Finance, and that all the others should be housed elsewhere. Many had moved out already, several to accommodation built for them, such as Yojana Bhavan (The House of Planning), Krishi Bhavan (The House of Agriculture) and so on. The rest were now also moved. The vast expansion of the public sector had added several offices to New Delhi. Even those companies with headquarters elsewhere, such as the Fertilizer Corporation at Bombay, or the Oil and Natural Gas Commission at Dehra Dun, maintained liaison offices and guest houses in Delhi. Almost all the state governments had representatives in the capital, with both office and residential accommodation for the many visitors from the states engaged in conducting business or extracting patronage and favour from the Union. New Delhi was bursting with the gigantic expansion of government activity and the many allied interests it attracted. With higher costs, both of land and building, the practice of building upwards was accelerated, and New Delhi no longer presented an elegant and orderly plan of single storey premises and gracious homes, private lawns and expanses of green public space. It was now patchy, with huge edifices visible everywhere.

The Ministry of Petroleum and Chemicals, located in 1967 at Shastri Bhavan, was a small organization by Union government standards. Its main responsibility was to formulate policy on and to administer the discovery, production, and distribution of crude oil, petroleum products and chemicals. This included the regulation of the private sector concerned with these commodities and the organization and control of a rapidly expanded public sector. It handled the delicate negotiations with the many foreign agencies controlling petroleum and chemical supplies and technology and the regulation of their activities.

India after independence had made giant strides towards technological competence and self-reliance in petroleum products. In 1948 consumption of these was small, 2.6 million tonnes; by 1971 it had gone up to

22.6 million. In 1947 India depended vitally on petroleum products imported from the Middle East by the major oil companies: in order of their scale of business, Burmah, Esso, and Caltex. There was a single small refinery at Digboi in Assam producing only 0.2 million tonnes of products and owned by the Burmah Oil Company through a subsidiary. This position of dependence was changed radically by petroleum policies influenced or formulated by K. D. Malaviya in his varying political capacities, including a period as minister, over the period 1952–63. The method mixed the nurturing and expansion of foreign know-how and interests with the limitation of their monopoly in order to achieve investment, knowledge, and control by Indians. Thus new refineries, working on imported crude oil, brought by the foreign companies from their own sources, were set up at Bombay (by Esso and Burmah Shell in 1954 and 1955) and Vizagapatam (by Caltex in 1957). India thus broke its dependence on imported petroleum products, though it still needed imported crude oil. Simultaneously action was initiated to set up further refineries under Indian control—in Gauhati (Assam) in 1962, Barauni (Bihar) 1964, Koyali (Gujarat) 1966 and Madras 1969. While each refinery involved foreign collaboration, the control was now Indian. The collaborators were Russian, Rumanian, American, and Iranian. In this way, by the end of the 1960s, India was manufacturing practically all its requirements of petroleum products and was able to run its own refineries. In this process collaboration of constructive value had also been established, particularly in the construction of pipelines, with ENI of Italy, a company in the public sector of that country.

For exploration, the Oil and Natural Gas Commission was established in the public sector in 1956, and in 1959 Oil India Limited was set up with equal shares between the government and the Burmah Oil Company for the exploration and production of crude in Assam. New finds were not of dramatic proportions, but India was producing 7.2 million tonnes in 1971 against 0.26 in 1948. For distribution the Indian Oil Corporation was set up in 1964, and by 1971 had gone over the 50 per cent mark in control of the retail market. The Indian Oil Company also ran the refineries in the public sector, producing products from indigenous crude, and was in a position to take over any expanded refinery capacity required in future. It is today indeed one of the giant corporations of the East and the only Indian company listed among the world's largest two hundred. Its profits in 1970–71 amounted to over twenty million rupees, the largest of all the ninety-seven public sector units. It is a shining, and unfortunately somewhat unique, exception in the ranks of these undertakings, many of which are running at a loss.

A start was made with the production of fertilizers (increased from

9,000 tonnes, in terms of nitrogen, in 1950–51 to 952,000 tonnes in 1971–72) and with the more sophisticated petrochemicals, especially plastics, synthetic fibres and synthetic rubber.

In this way by 1967, when I joined the ministry as Special Secretary, India had achieved and consolidated a break-through to knowledge, experience, and independence in both the production and the distribution of petroleum products. This had been done without alienating existing suppliers. The market was now shared, but the monopoly of knowledge and control had been eliminated.

The special secretary has identical powers, responsibility and position as the secretary to a ministry, though the latter is in overall coordinating charge and the final civil service adviser on policy to the minister. The designation of special secretary, among others, is a post-independence addition to the gradations of secretariat positions, and a reflection partly of the expanded activities of government, as also of the provision of new positions to provide the civil service with opportunities for advancement. The ministry was in charge of a minister of cabinet rank, in 1967 Mr Asoka Mehta, and a minister of state, Mr Raghu Ramiah. It had the usual gradation, below the secretary and special secretary, of joint secretaries, directors (a new position below joint secretary), deputy secretaries and under secretaries, with an office staff divided into sections, of about eight assistants and clerks, each in the control of a section officer, who had come up through the ranks of the secretariat. The ministry had only two, later three, joint secretaries, a key position often indicating the staff strength of a ministry. The Home ministry had as many as ten joint secretaries. This position in the Union government is in many ways a crucial position in the decision-making process; an officer above collector's rank, in the commissioner's scale of pay, the joint secretary is usually in charge of a group of allied, interconnected subjects, is permitted to deal direct with the minister, keeping his secretary informed on all important papers and orders, and is responsible for day-to-day administration. Moreover, in the Union secretariat, in contrast with that of the state, the secretary has a number of good senior level assistants and is relieved of much of the burden of detail. Once orders are given on a case, he seldom has to bother, except in a general way, about the follow-up of communications to the executives or other persons concerned to ensure their implementation. In a state even the chief secretary, on any delicate or complicated issue, may well have to draft detailed instructions for executives himself and repeatedly check that these have been followed. A secretary at the Union is able to involve himself, therefore, almost exclusively in policy formulation, negotiations with important outside interests, programmes for future development, and coordination between ministries.

Almost every problem, and even many of the individual communications dealt with in this ministry, had a technical content, and there was a small, though strong, team of technical officers. Relations between generalists and technical staffs were excellent. The exchanges between them were informal and not restricted by any conventions as to which officer, by reason of seniority or emoluments, had the right to approach which colleague for help, information, or guidance. In this matter the Petroleum and Chemicals Ministry was considered fortunate in comparison with other organizations where rather rigid practice determined the levels of exchange between generalist and technical officers.

Once policy on a subject was settled and defined, the ministry enjoyed considerable freedom in its enforcement, and important problems could be settled within it by the minister. Where, however, policy had not been definitely settled many coordinating agencies existed in the Union government for consultation. These included standing committees of officials, committees of the cabinet, and the cabinet itself. It is worth making some observations about their work as seen from the Ministry of Petroleum and Chemicals.

The parent ministry for industry was that of Industrial Development. All licensing cases and even those where an expansion of capacity was involved, went through the technical and administrative officers of the Petroleum and Chemicals Ministry to the Licensing Committee, headed by the secretary of the Industrial Development ministry and including representatives of the 'economic' ministries and technical experts. Once every quarter, and sometimes on an *ad hoc* basis, the Licensing Committee also included the directors of Industry of the state governments. The Licensing Committee approved a proposal, if it was within the terms of policy, or asked that it should be referred to the cabinet committee dealing with economic affairs, or more rarely, rejected the proposal altogether. It often asked for a review of particular aspects of the proposal.

A crucial wing of the Ministry of Industrial Development was that of the Director-General of Technical Development, a substantial organization of experts. Almost every licensing proposal had, on one point or another, to go to the Director-General of Technical Development before it could be put forward for approval. Of special importance were any proposals made for collaboration with a foreign party and the estimate of foreign exchange involved. The Director-General of Technical Development also had to be consulted when orders were proposed for equipment from abroad, even after a licence had been issued. This was a safeguard to limit the use of foreign exchange. The policy was that indigenous equipment would be preferred, even if more expensive. The issue was seldom as simple as that, however, because inevitably other problems also came up, such as the time it would take to manufacture a tailor-made item, its specifications and reliability, facilities for maintenance and servicing, the guarantees the manufacturer would give, and so on. There was considerable complaint on the part of both industrialists and the individual ministries concerned that there were delays in the many stages of processing. The defined aim was that a licence application should be settled within six months. This time limit was rarely achieved.

The ministry's relations with Finance, which were continuous, were coordinated by the appointment of a financial adviser, representing the Finance ministry, attached to the ministry itself. In case of disagreement between the financial adviser and the ministry the case went to the Finance ministry for their orders, and might if a *via media* could not be found proceed to the cabinet or its sub-committee for decision. An intelligent and sensitive financial adviser could be of invaluable assistance both in preventing extravagance or faulty expenditure, and in becoming the spokesman for the ministry in relations with Finance. The Finance ministry, apart from the financial adviser, had its own committees for considering particular aspects of industrial activity. The Foreign Investments Board under the chairmanship of the Finance secretary examined particularly whether proposals regarding sources from which finance would come were sound and appropriate.

The cabinet sub-committees received references for decision from the officials' committees or from the ministries. They did not invariably make a decision themselves but might well decide that the subject should go to the cabinet for consideration.

At civil service level the cabinet secretary, working directly with the Prime Minister, was the final coordinating authority. He was the head of the general 'committee of secretaries', as well as of that of the 'economic secretaries', as also of special committees dealing with aspects of defence, intelligence, and law and order. He was secretary to all the sub-committees of the cabinet. He was in this way exposed *ex officio* to all the most important coordinating memoranda, indeed responsible for their arrangement as agendas and decisions. He was also head of the department of personnel. He was thus able to acquire an almost instinctive feel for the total pattern and tone of policy in the government, functioning through its invariably more than a score of ministries.

Considerable time and effort in the ministry was devoted to dealings with and material for parliament. The procedures conformed generally to those of the British system and it is unnecessary to describe them. The significant point seems to be the contrast between the technically correct, though in fact rather cavalier and superficial, attention paid to the legislature in the state compared to the meticulous, hard worked, and exhaustive effort made by the administration, headed by their ministers, at the Union. A team of officers, headed by the secretary, was required to be present in the official gallery when the ministry's affairs were being discussed or questioned. Hastily scribbled notes would be sent to the minister if an instant reply was suddenly called for; otherwise, each point would be noted and a memorandum of explanation and comment given to the minister. On questions and possible supplementaries the minister would always do his homework with great diligence and care. Parliament was exacting business for both minister and officials. They were stretched in effort and in skill, the form and extent of the torture depending often on the time available for the particular process. Committees of parliament, and even communication and discussion with individual MPs, entailed somewhat similar strain.

The explanation for this attitude to parliament seems to lie partly in the tradition established by Pandit Nehru. His passion for the parliamentary system, even in the absence of a well-organized opposition, had made him insist on the greatest attention to even whispers of dissent, which often came from within his own party. Attention to parliament may also derive from the practical consideration that in the circumstances of India parliament is the best, indeed almost the only, mass medium available to an aspirant for all-India political recognition. Its proceedings and activities are automatically 'news' in all Indian papers, whatever their language, and, if significant, through all the radio broadcasts in all the regional languages. A state politician can and indeed must make his mark in his state substantially by personal contact and through his workers and propagandists. An all-India politician, even if he had the energy and time, cannot depend on personal contacts; he would be restricted by the language needed in various regions. Parliament is his main means of establishing an image and is of vital importance for political advancement; he must use the 'stage' of parliament to present, make known, and establish his credentials, to secure and advance his influence.

Thus in more than one way the practice of a great deal of government by discussion had developed in the Union secretariat, through the various and many coordinating committees of officials and of cabinet, the attention paid to debates, questions, and committees of parliament, and through *ad hoc* and informal exchanges between officials at all levels both within and between ministries. In fact one businessman, who had occasion to do work with the government, described the daily duties of an official in the Union as comprising 'meeting, eating and cheating'. He explained that when he wanted to contact an officer in the morning he invariably found that he was at a meeting, he had at midday taken a break for lunch; in the afternoon, facing his accumulated paper work and telephone messages, he was so tired and bewildered by the day's confabulations that all he could do for his client was to put him off in some way with a promise, 'cheating'.

In fact the system worked extremely efficiently in certain circumstances. Of this there was vivid experience during the 1971 war with Pakistan, following the long and painful unfolding of the Bangladesh episode. The Ministry of Petroleum and Chemicals was involved only at the fringes but did have to maintain the supply line of vital petroleum products and assist in the planning for their build-up. The business of government, in the many branches of activity requiring day-to-day coordination, and the frequent changes in operations following new events, was performed with speed and to constructive effect. The whole machinery worked as if its parts were highly lubricated and adapted to achieve their purpose.

That was not, however, the impression that the system made in the day-to-day work of government in the period 1967–71. Of this too there were several examples in the Petroleum and Chemicals ministry. One related to what was termed the 'big industrial houses'. It was the general policy of government that smaller units should be encouraged for new licensing rather than bigger ones, and particularly that monopolistic tendencies should be discouraged. This brought up the problem of performance and production. The country had, for example, attained self-sufficiency in caustic soda and soda ash. If this was to be maintained new production would have to be planned, licensed, and achieved to keep up with demand. The contradiction between speedy production and reliance on licensing new industrialists was allowed to drag on unresolved through a series of meetings and notings. It was in fact clear that, at least in the short term, demand could only be met by expanding larger units, in this case Tata's and Birla's, both 'big houses'. The country had again to start importing soda ash and caustic soda in 1970–71, and sizeable quantities in 1971–72. Suddenly expansion in the bigger units was then permitted. But meanwhile time, foreign exchange for imports, and clarity of policy positions had been lost while the process of decision-making dragged on.

This situation was symptomatic of a series of licensing cases in the ministry. Many petrochemicals, particularly synthetic fibres, are disproportionately responsive to economies of scale and it is impossible to achieve competitive and advantageous prices without big units of production. The choice between the practicality of size and the ideology of the small was to be 'solved' by resorting to the public sector enterprise. But a great deal of time and repetitive work was spent in contemplating the problem in relation to a number of individual cases, for the fact was that the public sector also raised many difficulties related to capacity, finances, and management. Its public image had been considerably tarnished by poor performance.

In this period there was also a crisis relating to crude oil prices. That these were, even in the 1960s, manipulated prices largely determined by the superstate of oil companies, is proved by the fact that crude prices went steadily but surely downwards in the period 1950 to 1970, a trend exactly opposite to the general inflation in prices. At the end of 1970 prices were jerked up significantly and a formula prescribed for periodic further increases. This indeed was a turning point in oil, and an indication that OPEC (the Organization of Petroleum Exporting Countries) had reached equality, indeed had even got the upper hand, in their relationships with the western oil companies. Events have now strengthened this power further. It was nevertheless clear even in 1970 that a crisis, even a revolution, in Middle East crude prices and supplies had taken place and essential control passed from the companies to the governments.

This was of vital concern to India, importing as she did two-thirds of her consumption, and with the fertilizer industry, on which depended the production of food, largely petroleum-based. Yet much of the ministry's efforts in meeting the situation were diverted and absorbed by a wrangle, based on historical and sentimental grounds, with the locally based foreign oil companies. Effort was directed to getting them to absorb the price increase, which proved futile and produced an impasse. The tussle was also unnecessary in any case, as the 'refinery agreements' with the companies were to end in a few years, at which time revision of terms where necessary could have been more appropriately sought. Instead the companies now pressed their view that as they did not see much future for their business in India the government should progressively take over their equity on suitable terms. These sets of problems led to many lengthy arguments, many conferences, and many papers, but did not assist in meeting the new situation in the crude market. In the process of revising and reconsidering old agreements with foreign companies, whose essential control of the supply position in India had already been loosened to an extent where it could even be eliminated if necessary, and in consequence of the delays and reservations in dealing with increased production by companies of the country, the government during this period lost a great deal of credibility and even respect, apart from critical and timely production.

What was the explanation of a state of affairs where the government was able to act with commendable, indeed skilful and masterly, efficiency in dealing with the special Bangladesh crisis, and yet unable to maintain orderly management of internal economic problems? This must be squarely attributed to the political climate at the time. Where the government was able to produce a clear objective and a determined policy, the administration worked well; where the policy was not clear and objectives became a subject of controversy, the administration even permitted the regular operations to deteriorate.

Congress split irrevocably in 1969, though signs and symptoms of the storm were evident after the 1967 general election, when it lost power in several states and gained only a small majority in the Union. During the struggle for power appeals were made to populist devices and programmes. The Communist Party of India became a virtual partner of 'Congress (R)', the 'new' ruling party, and exercised influence over its promises and actions. The image of radicalism permeated the posture of those in power, but was not translated into administratively practical programmes and concrete actions. An idea, a mere effervescence, passed for policy and became the current coinage of politics but it was not brought to earth; it was pervasive, never firmly pinned down.

This atmosphere had considerable influence on administrative arrangements in the Union secretariat. A system of work by discussion and conference had no doubt been developed partly to aid quick decisions. Now it was used to avoid them. Conferencing became the opportunity to voice various possiblities, points of view, and apparent contradictions between departments and ministries. Often all that emerged was the decision that further enquiries should be made, and that another group of persons, often experts, should examine the problem.

Nor did discussion reduce the quantity and burden of paper work. Indeed the Government of India had always had meticulous habits of most extensive recording. As decisions now took a great deal of time, passing through several channels, memoranda tended to accumulate considerable histories. On controversial subjects, in circumstances where the line of action between possible alternatives was not clear, and particularly where there might be scope to assess an opinion as too much to the 'right' and not in keeping with the mood of current politics, memoranda now included copies of all the preceding discussions, so that no adverse conclusion or selective editing could be made. For similar reasons the profusion of conferences and writing often failed to produce clearly defined points of view and differences of opinion between officials and ministries. On the other hand, effort was directed at achieving a 'consensus', a trend of emphasis, rather than defined indications of disagreement or action. The attempt was directed to producing a harmony of acceptable material, which was sometimes more easily done by slurring over, rather than defining, inherent contradictions or genuine practical difficulties.

Indeed it was surprising how quickly the secretariat shed its habit of individual pin-pointed notes by officials, discussing various alternatives and defining a recommendation as to the best solution in the opinion of the writer. Many notes, particularly on controversial subjects, were now mere records of a discussed point of view, rather than acceptances of responsibility by the individuals in the hierarchy for a specific proposal by which they stood and which was on record. There was an inevitable softening of sharp differences, a failure to bring out clearly the strengths and weaknesses of alternative courses. The aim now was to find the smooth, often at the cost of not even dealing with the pragmatic or the practical. There was an undercurrent of fear that frank opinion, should it go against the dominant trend which remained undefined in practical detail, might bring adverse consequences for the individual. The government did not receive, and apparently did not want, independent advice from its officials.

This experience suggests that the quality and character of the administrative decision-making apparatus is crucially dependent on political direction, and the values held and displayed by the political masters.

10

PATTERNS OF ADMINISTRATIVE CHANGE

Chapters 2 to 9 have broadly limited themselves to a description of the administration at work in various spheres, in areas as different as the Punjab and Jammu and Kashmir, and more briefly at the Union. Aspects of change in institutional arrangements and in administrative methods that seemed to emerge directly from the subjects considered have been mentioned, and on occasion a problem or question suggested.

This chapter defines more specific changes in the style and methods of Indian administration related to both organizational arrangements and their impact on the judgements and views of citizens and civil servants. This includes more controversial ground, and many of the conclusions suggested are not provable fact; different opinions might well be credibly held. A degree of surmise and assessment is involved.

It is not possible to portray a wholly consistent picture of the process of change as directed to a defined end and objective. The forces that play on Indian administration and determine the texture of government reveal no definite order, and have not achieved a stability of form or discipline, nor a clear line of command. The whole situation is not a pattern but literally a mix, a mass of ingredients in the process of change. These are therefore in the nature of a series of pictures rather than a single composition. Such general conclusions as are drawn suggest tendencies and potentials rather than firm landmarks of arrival or departure. The Indian administrative system still poses many fundamental issues that remain finally undetermined, even though the institutional forms through which these are expressed, or to which they are related, are recognizable, indeed familiar and firm. However diverse the manifestations, on one point in post-independence Indian administration there has been no doubt. The fact of the universal vote has had to be reckoned with and considered in all administrative policy. The political master has been sensitive to the requirement that at least every five years he must return to his voter for a new lease of power or a refusal of it.

DECLINE IN THE IMPORTANCE OF THE DISTRICT OFFICER

At independence the district officer, with his district as the basic operative unit in the administration, dominated the scene. This is no longer so today, and the importance of both the district and the district officer has weakened, even disintegrated. Many causes have led to this change.

The vast expansion of government activities, particularly in the economic sphere, both at the Union and in the states, has in perspective reduced the district to smaller size; it has been cut in proportion. The district officer himself is no longer the almost exclusive dispenser of government patronage and power in his jurisdiction. He has to contend daily with the forces, personalities, and prejudices of public opinion, which are backed by, and are the eventual creators of, political power. The district officer has to deal with the MP, the MLA, and the local political and social bosses. He must discuss, persuade, cajole and at times evade. He is by no means the near-exclusive source of information or influence within the government in regard to the policies and decisions he is required to implement.

The MLA is generally not concerned with the broad issues of policy. But with regard to his constituency, he is avidly interested in working upon the district authorities in the cause of securing response to the demands made by local people. Many of these demands are centred round the character and activities, the decisions and sometimes the manners, of the district personnel. Local politicians often use the word 'accommodating' not in a derogatory sense but to praise a local officer; the opposite idea is conveyed in the phrase 'not caring for the public'. The district officer is under constant seige to 'accommodate' the wishes of influential members of the public in a variety of matters, such as the posting of personnel to particular places, the obtaining of permits and licences of a discretionary kind, and the redress of grievances. The MLA is interested in future power; his presence is therefore felt and his voice heard on subjects that are the cause of unrest, like communal (religious) tension, labour troubles; discipline and morale in educational institutions. Wherever a significant number of people are involved, he has to make himself heard. Much of this activity is not, in its manner of conduct, orderly. A great deal of it is uneven, unorganized and shaped by occasion; it entails persuasion and pressure and is expressed in meetings, conversations and contacts with citizens, officials and fellow politicians up to ministerial level. It is listening, discussing, pleading, arguing. In the MLA's relations with officials there is commonly a barely concealed hint that he enjoys or can secure the backing of party chiefs or members of government.

The district officer thus competes for the validity and acceptance of his decisions; these are constantly under fire. This may well be inevitable, even useful, in a democracy. But circumstances have progressively weakened his capacity to compete. Compared to his pre-independence predecessor, he lacks experience and knowledge of the problems and people with whom he deals. Several factors have contributed to this comparative weakness. With the expansion of government, he spends a much shorter span of his career in districts; nor does he regard this period as the very heart of his career. It is often merely a stepping stone to a move elsewhere. An ambitious and able officer will now spend only three or four of his thirty or more service years in the districts; his predecessors spent a good half of their time in them. The opportunity, indeed the need, to get steeped in the local environment, in the ways and moods of people in villages, has largely disappeared. This process has been aided and abetted by the virtual disappearance of the horse as the essential means of mobility. The jeep is now the district officer's way of travel. This usually enables him to visit even the farthest end of his district, perform his duties there, and return by evening to head-quarters, or at least to some town where creature comforts and the society of his own kind are available. The days and nights of rest house touring are a phenomenon of the past. With this kind of travel has also gone the opportunity, in informal and comparatively slow, but infinitely more familiar and effective, ways, of getting to know the people and their problems. It is ironic that a vehicle of comparative speed like the jeep has accelerated a process of increasing ignorance rather than deeper knowledge. Old customs die hard in India, and even though both district and horse have declined in importance—the latter indeed has all but disappeared—the IAS is still taught riding, and some period of service in a district is regarded as essential to an officer's prospects. An outward and visible sign of the new situation is that the District Gazetteer is no longer revised by the district or settlement officer. An official, selected for his economic and academic back-ground, sits at state headquarters to perform this function, though he may well collect data from the districts.

Another consequence of this situation is that positions at the sec-retariat rank higher than those in a district. It is the aim of the ambitious officer to achieve a position in the former as early as possible. The number of places available, at all levels of service, has multiplied greatly, which also makes it easier to attain this ambition. The secretariat is to some degree insulated from the direct rough and tumble of politics, and enjoys all the fuller amenities, social, educational, and material, of the capital of the state. The lure of the secretariat has be-come dominant among the career values of civil servants. Allied with it are the many opportunities now available for 'headquarters' jobs in the state capital—not in the secretariat itself but in the several specialized organizations of the government, particularly in the economic sphere. Beyond this level of course are the positions in both the Union sec-retariat and its affiliated institutions. With rare exceptions, it is now only the second-raters who spend prolonged or repeated periods working as district officers, or even as commissioners of divisions.

THE 'STEEL FRAME' HAS GONE

Along with the decline of the district there has been a loosening of the grip on the whole administration by the top administrative service, the ICS and its successor the IAS. Chapter 2 describes how the ICS dominated the administrative machine. In Chapter 7 reference has been made to influences that have weakened the strength and image of the IAS. The IAS now has no vital link with the judiciary, which is an independent organization. The importance of this change is not that it has deprived the IAS of an avenue of promotion, nor even that they have lost an opportunity for experience in the interpretation of the law. Rather it is that administrators are now judged in courts of law by judges who have no experience themselves of the difficulties, responsibilities or even the temptations of administrative work.

It may be argued that a complete separation of hitherto common experience between executive and judiciary is salutary in both principle and fact. Nevertheless this is a new administrative situation in India, which perhaps has not yet had sufficient experience in self-governing institutions to build a bridge of comprehension and constructive interchange between the two branches of government. These processes are being worked out and may well take some years to achieve. Meanwhile the judge delivers his dispensation and passes to the next; the administrator faces the consequences in his arena.

The integral and built-in dependence between the police and the civil authorities has also disappeared and further weakened the concentrated command and authority of the IAS. The police, for reasons already touched on, tend to become of special importance to the political leadership in the states. Both Partap Singh Kairon in the Punjab and Bakshi Ghulam Mohammad in Jammu and Kashmir had a 'special relationship' with the police force, utilized not only for law and order but also for political, administrative and patronage objectives. The police have no vital dependence, as they had previously, on the help of the civil authority, and, when occasion or the disposition of the political master provokes, can easily be used as an independent instrument of power, not on the effective leash of normal civilian control. The police are certainly under *political* control, but the administrative and legal institutional arrangements no longer provide the means by which they are yoked inextricably, at crucial stages of the administrative process, with civil authority and influence. They are now more easily unyoked for exclusively political direction. This unyoking has been a recurring problem in various parts of India; it is difficult to avoid the conclusion that it is inherent in the revised administrative set-up, and not merely a matter of chance, personality, or accident.

A new and less well-knit relationship has developed between the main civil services and the technical establishments. In regard to management positions in government the defined policy remains as it was. The government may choose for management positions personnel from the IAS or from the specialist services. For example, secretaries to government for branches of the Public Works department are usually from the administrative services. The managing directors of public sector companies have been more mixed, sometimes specialists and often generalists. But considerable claims have developed on the part of the technical services as to their relations with the administrative services. Argument and debate continue. The present position is uneasy and may well demand fresh regulation. Some changes in practice have already taken place.

The two main claims of technical personnel relate to powers and salaries. Technical personnel have increasingly insisted that all posts with a primarily technical function, even management positions, should be manned by technical officers. Much of this dispute has centred round the statutory electricity board, which each sizeable state, sometimes a group of them, sets up to manage the production and distribution of electricity. The membership core of each board comprises engineering personnel, but there are usually some non-official members and the chairman has often been a generalist. In recent years the appointment of a non-technical chairman has met with resistance, even at times (as in UP and Delhi) with organized agitation going as far as suspected sabotage. While the government has not by definition conceded the principle, it has in fact in the case of these two states appointed technical officers to replace those from the administrative services.

Engineering personnel also claim that their salary scales should be the same in respect of increment amounts and intervals as those prescribed for the IAS. They refer also to 'time-bound' promotions from one level to a higher, so that each officer has a guarantee of achieving a defined rank within a known period. The mood of large numbers in the technical services, particularly the engineers, is one of extreme sensitiveness with reference to their comparative position in the government and even their rights as individuals. In Punjab a recent phase of this feeling rallied round the chairman of the electricity board, an engineer, whose house had been searched, and ancillary action taken, on a suspicion of corruption. This became an occasion for engineering personnel of the board, and of the neighbouring states of Delhi and UP acting in sympathy, to threaten to slow down, even stop, the flow of electricity. The Punjab government had to compromise; they did not, as they apparently wished to do, suspend the chairman, pending enquiry into his conduct. He continued and so did the enquiry.

Problems relating to the technical services have large implications, considering the vast expansion of technical activities, India's crucial need of progress in this realm, and the large number of public sector companies engaged in production, where technical operations are the hard core of the enterprise. Whereas in these companies there has so far not been any organized agitation to secure appointments, or promotions, for technical officers, there are indications of pressure to achieve these. This has helped on occasion to produce phenomenal delays in making appointments. For example, in the Petroleum and Chemical Ministry the post of chairman, Oil and National Gas Commission was vacant for three years with a stop-gap arrangement.

The ramifications and development of government have set the stage and on occasion even created the need for greater autonomy for technical personnel. The old relationship of control at critical points by the generalist administrator is the subject of heated debate and of unrest and untidiness. Many of the problems that have been raised remain unresolved and new dispensations may well be forced.

In these pressures the loss of the intimate association of the ICS (now the IAS) with the idea of the district has also played its part. The district had been the symbol of the civil servant's profession. The ICS officer possessed a distinctive value based on his continuous detailed contact with the mass of the people in the district. It was on the credentials of this hard core of experience that he performed on other related platforms of government, but in professional repute he stood unrivalled on ground of his own. That link no longer exists, and he lacks the essential core of a professionalism peculiarly his own. He may in the process have gained many more opportunities in new areas of government, but with that has also come a degree of anonymity, which makes him less distinctive in competing for position and power with other branches of the civil services.

The cumulative influence of these forces, and other aspects of the same kind of development mentioned later, has caused steady erosion of one of the main features of the Indian administration, the massive prestige and the comprehensive impact of the main civil service. This is quite definitely no longer 'the steel frame'.

PUBLIC ATTITUDES

Public and political reactions, values, judgements, and even sentiments and prejudices represent the crucial context for the government's work in a democracy and influence directly and palpably the morale of the administration. These represent a complex and intricate pattern of forces in India, and only a somewhat disjointed and selective account of a few items that stand out is attempted here. Every activity and each institution of government acts and reacts with public opinion or feeling, so that the points discussed here are by no means intended to imply that there is not a public opinion content to other matters which are not mentioned.

(i) Suspicion of Bureaucracy

A reaction against authority and suspicion of bureaucrats is in varying degree the common experience of humanity. In a colonially ruled country the feeling goes deep; it is certainly part of the air that every Indian breathes. Even India's bureaucrats are suspicious of bureaucracy, its politicians more so. The government was foreign and may also be devilish. That was prevalent sense and feeling in British times. At independence, however, substantial palliatives helped to curb extreme opinion. The manner of transfer of power from British to Indians was highly cooperative. It was preceded by a struggle for independence which achieved the character and inspiration of a moral challenge. Credit for this goes to Mahatma Gandhi and the British, both of whom eventually accepted the position that freedom for India should be assessed in terms of human rights rather than weighed on the scales of all-out violence. These features permitted a treaty of transfer which among other items preserved the security, the conditions of service, and the integrity of the civil service. Nevertheless, deeply ingrained in the historic memory and instinctive reflexes of the Indian citizen there remained a suspicion of government and of the civil service. Manifestations of this have been pervasive and important in independent India.

It is generally accepted Indian morality that cheating the government is fair enough. Businessmen with the highest standards of professional morality in their dealings with each other and their customers do not think twice about filching from the government. The gloves are off, and the only restraints are often the danger of exposure and defeat. It is only this attitude which explains the dimension of transactions in what is called 'black money', which is today assessed by all experts as in effect constituting a parallel economy. This money evades the account books and the taxation system. India has for several years presented the contradiction of having the highest taxation rates in the world, and yet producing the most affluent display of conspicuous consumption by a minority. The government is everybody's milch cow in independent India; you take from it what you can.

The malady of suspicion however goes even deeper. The political masters have accepted the civil service as a necessary evil but have taken great care not to identify themselves with it. This separateness and suspicion has been a fact of significance in some of the decisions mentioned in previous chapters. The name ICS was dropped in favour of IAS; in community development, it was decided not to use the existing revenue agency for mass contact; the decontrol of food, palpably premature in 1948, was decided on at least partly because of the suspicion of the civil service as corrupt participators in controls.

(ii) *The Duality of the Indian Mind*

Most human beings, perhaps particularly the more aspiring, carry the burden of at least two characters within them: the one stretching out to achieve the desirable and the ideal, the other squaring this aspiration with the hard realities of what the environment permits. We are as individuals and as communities forever catching up with ourselves in finding a balance between dream and reality. That is the essence of the human predicament; the associative capacity of man enables him to build edifices from pieces of past experience, castles in the air, and his zeal for knowledge and excellence compels him to convert these to the facts of life. He does so to some extent, only to find that arrival is merely the base for a new vista that tantalizes him yet again. Man is both privileged and doomed to endless effort.

Indian history, including as it does a series of invasions, conquests, and waves of religious persecution, has gone far to produce what, for lack of a better term, may be called 'the duality of the Indian mind'. Matthew Arnold put it in romantic terms:

> The East bow'd low before the blast
> In patient deep disdain;
> She let the legions thunder past
> And plunged in thought again.

The results are less romantic. Here is a culture and society that in spite of repeated subjugation, the last phase of which was British colonial rule, has survived for thousands of years. There are Indians today performing acts, social and religious, trivial or important, in exactly the same way as their forefathers did over the centuries. India survived by developing a second skin, living in two worlds even for ordinary purposes. It has become normal reflex with most Indians to perform all the functions, even embellishments, of conformity with the regime around them, and yet practise and believe in clandestine privacy, often isolated, at other times within their group, values of their own.

Duality has served India well as a means and instrument of survival. Without it Indian culture would have lost its identity and been absorbed and merged. It has made duality, however, a part of the Indian character. The two worlds in which he has so continuously lived need never meet within the Indian; they have survived for long as two independent self-revolving circles. With independence and democracy the decks were cleared for bringing both together in integrated, practical strength. The habit of duality, however, persists and creates great problems which influence administration. There is a divorce from reality, a tendency not to link cause necessarily with effect, rather to sustain both independently of each other, to work and judge in a vacuum. It is possibly one of the greatest tragedies of foreign rule that a whole society loses the instinct and the feel of the inevitability and rhythm of reality.

Administrative policy and activity take place against this background. Programmes are quite often decided upon, and judged, without any measure of what is workable and practical, and therefore without any commitment or attempt to accept the compromises and restraints involved. When they do not work as imagined and planned the administration is frequently made the scapegoat in the vacuum that remains.

An example may be seen in the working of land reforms, to which the Congress party was committed long before independence and to which it directed detailed legislation immediately on assuming power. More than twenty-five years after the event there is dissatisfaction with the distribution of land and governments are continually reaffirming their decision to enforce land legislation with speed and thoroughness. This contradiction between avowed and determined objective and reality occurs at least partly because facts in the field have not been made to match with the definitions of the law. The shades and shadows of duality have confused and bedevilled enforcement.

The food monopoly of 1973–74 (described in Appendix I) has substantial elements of duality in practice. The motivation that sustained the contradiction in it seems to have been to oust the trade by establishing a monopoly in grain but to avoid rationing. When this collapsed, it was proclaimed an administrative failure, not the consequence of pursuing faulty policy.

In dealing with, and judging, the administration, Indian opinion reverts to its habits of old, of looking at it and assessing it as an external influence, even an infliction, and not as a part and parcel of its own governance of itself.

The point may be considered from another angle in the telling statement made by Morarji Desai, MP, a previous Union finance minister, commenting in mid-1973 on the bleak outlook in India. He said ‘*Hum to apni asanion men phans gai*’ (‘we have got enmeshed in the ease with which we have been surrounded’). He apparently had in mind that India achieved freedom with ease, without a fight to the last ditch, which would have created for it a sense of reality. India’s achievement of freedom from the British was a denouement of good morals, almost of good manners, no doubt a great credit to each of the two countries involved, but nonetheless it left the vacuum of unreality unfilled by the experience of the people.

Much of the outstanding success of Gandhi's leadership may well have lain in combining the duality of the Indian mind with programmes of practical action. He achieved the unique distinction of conferring self-respect on Indians of all classes of society while still under foreign rule. He insisted that freedom was a matter of morality, not of force; it was an idea of yourself; he raised duality to transcend the inconvenient facts of British power and the British presence. In doing so he achieved a mass surge of organization, essential decency, and brave aspiration determined to attain the fact of freedom, without the fact, without in India's case even the possibility, of force. But he went beyond this. He put to the Indian people tasks and programmes of a limited practical kind. The insistence on spinning and the exclusive use of home-made cloth is an example, involving a simple set of actions each person could perform, and which defined an immediate, practical challenge to his time, energy, and zeal. Perhaps Gandhi's economic programmes, which came later to be known derisively as 'Gandhian economics', looked at in the context of India's history, had a bigger significance than they are credited with for the growth of an experienced and integrated citizenship.

(iii) *The Judiciary*
Two branches of the public service, the army and the judiciary, have gained in public respect and esteem since independence. By contrast, the administration, close to the firing line of public contact in expanding government activity, has lost considerable ground.

A consequence of this generally held public reaction is that on any controversial action the relevant pressure groups, and the affected public, usually demand a judicial investigation. Even in the normal course of administration many decisions are subject to examination by the courts. This is indeed essential, but the Indian public also demands that where an event or act has roused public indignation, suspicion, or strong feelings, it should be examined by a commission of enquiry under the chairmanship of a judge. The occasions when such commissions are set up by the governments of the states, and at the Union, have increased considerably since independence. They deprive the administrators of the judgement of their peers, and place them in the hands of strangers to executive responsibilities.

It is conceded that there are occasions and situations where facts should be established, to public satisfaction and for remedial measures, by persons immune from the suspicion of executive bias, yet it must also be realized that the indiscriminate, or frequent, use of such procedure puts a grave burden on the administrator who at times suffers harassment and anxiety to an extent that confidence and initiative might be impaired. There are also indications that ministers sometimes accept the appointment of a commission to avoid immediate embarrassment and debate on the floor of the house, as the existence of a commission puts the subject behind the cloak of the *sub judice*. The time-lag created in this way often divests the subject of much of its venom and thrust.

It seems worthwhile to examine some occasions where a commission was appointed and the consequences that followed. The Commission of Inquiry (1964) into allegations against Chief Minister Partap Singh Kairon comprised a single judge, S. R. Das, retired from the Supreme Court. It reported in a matter of seven months, finding Kairon guilty on some of the issues with reference to the misuse of power and influence to benefit his sons and their friends. Kairon quit. A similar subject was invoked in the Commission comprising Mr Justice Ayyengar, also a retired judge of the Supreme Court, investigating allegations against Bakshi Ghulam Mohammad, who had been chief minister of Jammu and Kashmir. The Commission reported in June 1967, within twenty-eight months of appointment. Some of the phenomenal delay was due to the tactics adopted by Bakshi who finally refused to appear before the Commission. Bakshi was found guilty on charges more serious than Kairon though on a similar theme. He had already been forced out of office in 1964, and the public evinced little interest in the report.

Both these commissions, which involved top ministers in the states, without doubt looked into matters of 'urgent public importance' which phrase summarizes the intention of the Commission of Inquiry Act. It is, however, in cases lower down the line, involving members of the administrative services, that perhaps less satisfactory justification for the use of the commission exists.

In October 1966 the police opened fire at Jammu on a mob of provocatively violent students who had also committed arson. Several were injured and three persons killed. The police were also badly mauled. A Commission, comprising Judge Mukerji, retired from the Allahabad High Court, assisted by two district judges, reported in May 1967, commenting most adversely on the executive. The report was replete with eloquent clichés and aspirations as to how the public, and students particularly, should be dealt with, and its very language and contents were evidence of its essentially academic and window-dressing character. The officials concerned were then charged as individuals and put on the mat of departmental enquiry by the government. They in fact got away substantially unscathed in the detailed enquiry against them, but a long period of harassment was involved. A similar result may well have been obtained without the procedure of a Commission, which it seems obvious was established in this case to meet the upsurge of public feeling, and to gain time for tempers to cool.

A more complicated case was when 'the Ganges caught fire', as the newspaper reports described it. The Barauni refinery is located near the river and, though an arrangement of syphons and canals discharges effluent into it, under a technical arrangement that ensures a mix with the waters within permissible limits of pollution. The river flows down to the city of Monghyr, where the scum on an inlet was noticed to be burning one day in April 1968. The water supply in the city had to be diverted for some days to deal with the situation. A Commission of Inquiry, headed by Manohar Parshad, retired chief justice of the Patna High Court, with two technical members, held in July 1969 that the management of the refinery carried prime responsibility for the occurrence. The general manager was a generalist of the IAS who had apparently brought to the notice of his engineers defects he had observed, as a layman, in some of the units of the factory. He was none-theless held guilty by the Commission but was finally cleared in early 1973, four years after the report, after the detailed departmental enquiry into the case.

Commissions of Inquiry often take a great deal of time to report. The Trombay Commission of Inquiry, looking into allegations about fertilizer factories, set up in August 1969, had not reported even after three years and the Pipelines Commission, also concerned with the Ministry of Petroleum and Chemicals, set up in August 1970 had not reported in early 1974. Indeed there is evidence to suggest that the use of retired judges, which is the almost invariable practice, tends to prolong investigation. Most lawyers at the Union level are paid fees per hearing. The prospect of a prolonged swelling of fees is not likely to induce any grave urgency or speed. If in addition to this the retired judge also enjoys an extended period of full pay and amenities the temptation to sift evidence most meticulously is hardly unexpected. The suggestion that retired judges should be paid a lump sum, fixed in advance, for an enquiry has not thus far found favour.

The whole question of subjecting executive acts to judicial fact-finding investigation bristles with difficulties, and in the developments that have taken place in this direction since independence there is scope for the evolution of custom, convention, and usage to secure both the public interest and security and the continued confidence and initiative of the executive agencies

(iv) *Vigilance*

Every chief minister, on taking up his position, or when he gets a renewed mandate from the electorate and his party, announces in his statement of objectives, usually high up on the list, a determination to 'root out corruption'. The public is obviously greatly interested and concerned about graft in the administrative system. It is certainly generally believed that there is corruption. Complaints are voiced, with reference to particular events and even persons, by MPs, MLAs, and in the press. Even among the services there are few individual officials who would maintain that public life is generally clean; many hold the opposite view.

No doubt as a result of this feeling, organizations and special arrangements for dealing with cases have been set up since independence and have proliferated greatly. Anti-corruption institutional arrangements, now usually called 'vigilance' in official parlance, are a marked development. While types of organization in the states vary, there is in almost every one a vigilance commissioner, usually of higher seniority than an ordinary secretary, assisted by a special police cell, headed often by a deputy inspector-general, and with extraordinary powers to call for papers and to interrogate officials and people. This organization is almost always included in the chief minister's portfolio, working either directly under him or through the chief secretary. At the Union there is a central vigilance commissioner, similarly empowered, and entitled to enlist the help of the Central Bureau of Investigation (CBI), the highest intelligence group in the country. The central vigilance commissioner is required to be consulted by ministries and departments at appropriate stages of any case where corruption may be suspected.

The results achieved are in terms of statistics negligible, though the number of complaints made and cases investigated is large. Does this mean that there is little corruption, or are there other explanations?

Procedures are often blamed for lack of performance in bringing cases to the point of 'a kill'. It is true that these provide the fullest opportunity to the suspect for producing a defence; there are also avenues of appeal and review; for serious punishments consultation with the relevant Public Service Commission is required. It is doubtful, however, whether procedures can be blamed so much as the lack of a defined, generally accepted, public opinion as to what amounts to punishable corruption. It is possibly because the social cement, the interpretation, and the will are inadequately cohesive that corruption remains unproven and punishments are few and far between. When it comes to evidence the public is often apathetic, sometimes even afraid. The investigating agency does not receive credible support from reliable objective sources.

The important question still remains whether there is sizeable corruption or not. A categorical answer is hardly possible. Some observations which throw light on the issue may be permitted. The kind of tipping mentioned in Chapter 2 certainly continues all through the administration, at the lower levels probably on a scale more general and higher than before, in view of the extension of government and inflation. This, however, does not amount to corruption in the sense of decisions made, withheld, or delayed because of money.

The extent of corruption varies considerably with the character of the top political leadership. The careers of both Partap Singh Kairon and Bakshi Ghulam Mohammad suggest that it is at its worst when there is a link in corruption, and an active operational relationship, between politician and official. This situation also creates fear that the administration can be used for personal gain at the highest level, and that it would be foolish and hazardous to expose it. It creates suspicion, so that even *bona fide* actions, which displease particular persons, tend to be highlighted by them in an atmosphere already charged with the belief that evil exists and is tolerated. A significant manifestation of the link between politician and administration has been the growing belief of the late 1960s and early 1970s that the Congress Party in power has depended greatly on clandestine contributions extracted by it from people, mostly in industry and controlled trades, who do business with the government.

At no time since independence have the public believed that the administration was completely clean, but the extent of suspicion has varied considerably. Over the years, however, and particularly in the later period, the belief that there is corruption has grown rather than diminished.

The increase in the procedures and subjects of licensing and permits has created large inspectorate level staffs. It is widely held that they are paid routine retainers by the business community to avoid harassment and that these are increased on occasions where any discretionary extra facility is involved. With many of these activities, as also in the matter of route permits used by truck drivers, including ancillaries such as overloading, trespassing into territory covered by another route, and the like, the police are the pervasive common denominator as far as the ultimate sanction of the law goes. They are participators in both routine retainers and *ad hoc* extras from the relevant public. Where corruption becomes a routine system, its eradication is even more difficult as any attempt to do so meets with the clandestine, yet strong and united, resistance of the whole vested interest which benefits from it. The honest official becomes a target for highly organized attack from within his own administration.

The paraphernalia of vigilance has become an important factor influencing the action, initiative, and awareness of the administrator today. He is conscious of being watched, of possible pitfalls in what he may do. This tends to diminish his vigour, make him cautious and curb his discretion to meet difficulty with pragmatic improvised manoeuvre; he plans for safety by reducing a great deal to writing and evidence rather than taking quick and effective action. It is the honest official with no political base or relationship, who becomes the more cautious operator; the dishonest merely assess the risks involved and may raise their fees! In this way administrative processes tend, especially at grass-roots level where they meet the bulk of their clients, to lose efficiency, speed, and the use of that marginal discretion often required to meet fully the needs of a particular case. Whatever else vigilance may have achieved, it has certainly made government slower, less satisfying to its clients, and less efficient in adaptation. Obviously more difficult solutions, in the moral and social sphere, must be found to deal with corruption.

(v) *The Public Servant in Action*

While the extent of corruption in public administration may well be debatable, on the question of whether the government, particularly at the point at which it makes daily contact with the people, is sensitive, courteous and satisfying, there can be less doubt over most of the post-independence period. It must be assessed as insensitive and unsatisfactory.

The tradition of Indian society and administrators, literally over centuries, has been that government, at all levels, conveyed 'orders'. The concept of the 'public servant' even in its broadest sense has hardly existed. There have been notable exceptions in the ranks of Indian rulers. Asoka spread a benevolent, almost missionary, hegemony over a great part of what is India and Pakistan before Christ. Akbar, the greatest of the Mughal emperors, enjoyed a high reputation contemporaneously for standards of governance in the matter of certainty of system and procedure for his citizens. Substantially, however, authority and its minions have been something apart from and above the people.

This tradition changed somewhat during British rule, when law and defined procedure eventually determined relations between citizens and government and greater mobility assisted uniformity in performance. But the fact remains that British administrators were also regarded, both by Indians and the British themselves, not only as public servants but also and more so, in crisis crucially so, as emissaries, representatives, and repositories of British authority, policy, and power. They were enveloped, sustained, and nourished in the trappings of 'prestige', as a body of special men called upon to perform special functions to ensure justice and good order, indeed to confer these privileges on the subjects of the British Raj. As a small and harmless example of this feeling, I recall sending up to my English superior a draft on rationing which included a sentence urging equality of treatment. Among the categories of privileged, who must be treated on a par with the rest of the public I had included 'landlords, *nawabs*, *pukka sahibs*', etc. My superior swallowed the draft but cut out the *'pukka sahibs'* who obviously should not be brought into the arena of the everyday.

The tradition of authority had its counterpart in the attitude of the people. Indeed it is difficult to analyse which came first in the process. The Indian has regarded his rulers—perhaps a more accurate term to use than public servants—as persons in chosen positions of power, the dispensers of authority conferred by the King, the Court, or the Governor. Attitudes have included fear, awe and acceptance, gratitude if authority was fair or generous, acquiescence if it was not. They have been accompanied by flattery, subservience, a bolstering of egos and vanities rather than a levelling of them.

It is only with independence, and to some extent during the struggle for it, that the idea of the public servant at last took root and became a rationale for practice. Indeed immediately following independence there were several indications that both officials and non-officials were changing their attitudes and actions to meet the new circumstances. Some flavour and temper of this change persists. The ideas of the constitution and the laws are basically inspired by this concept of the administrator as a public servant.

Custom and usage, however, respond but slowly and fitfully. The working of bureaucracy continues to reveal the substance of past tradition in this matter. In daily working the civil servant exhibits few of the signs of a public servant. In most offices the official transacts business as if he is conferring a boon, a favour, on his client. Even a ration card is looked on less as a right of the citizen than almost a gift of the administration. The client gets few services across the counter in a normal Indian office. He may have a long wait; when he receives attention it rarely concentrates on achieving a full answer for him. He is often asked to come again, and generally to provide further information 'in writing'.

Most of the officers, who have the authority to pass final orders, are heavily dependent on clerks. The officer will usually wait till the client's problem comes to him on paper. There is little finality in direct customer contact. The customer also tends to curry favour with the clerk. There is much coming and going; the paraphernalia of decision is multitudinous, often confusing. Much of this has become a way of life to officials and go-betweens like lawyers. It affords them psychological satisfaction, social contact, and status. It has a life of its own. While it is true that an Indian official is rarely so heartless as to say a peremptory 'no' to a request, it is also true that extracting a 'yes', or some degree of it, will take a great deal of time. With these methods of work go flattery and a seeking of relationships to obtain attention and the service or dispensation sought. The whole idea of what in India is commonly called 'approach' is developed and catered for in a variety of ways and through many possible intermediaries. It may be a relation, a friend, or someone with authority over the official. In decisions where discretion is involved the seeking of a suitable 'approach' often precedes or accompanies the presentation of a claim.

The system also inevitably produces the other side of the medal, which is the speed and ease with which performance emerges when the client is powerful or influential. The lubrication provided by such a personality removes all rigidity and the decision may well be quick, courteous, and meticulous in detail. Is it surprising that the Defence minister, Jagjivan Ram, forgot all about his income tax for almost a decade with no untoward action or result? This in turn causes suspicion and lack of confidence among the ordinary clientele; it again reaffirms the belief that 'approach' is essential. There is thus a vicious circle, a snowballing malaise. Almost every Indian in a public office is not only a victim but also a perpetrator and carrier of the disease.

Nor does the Indian citizen often enjoy the spectacle and experience of a well-ordered, neat, and clean public office. These are usually both disorderly and unclean. They are littered with bundles of dishevelled paper that have often collected both dust and vermin; the floors are invariably dirty, tables covered with the accretions of several days' business—ink stains, paper, cigarette ends, and the stains of *pan* (betel nut potions). This further enhances the gloom, apprehension, and help-lessness that often characterize citizens' contacts with public offices, particularly those, such as the *tehsil* level, which deal with a sizeable body of them.

It is difficult to apportion blame as between officials and public. The attitudes, values, and pressures of both act and react on each other to produce a mix that certainly lacks vigour, efficiency, and service. There are, of course, exceptions but India has not yet caught up with the idea or the reality of the public servant. The government is far from being consumer-conscious at the daily administrative level, though it is so at the level of power and politics. The Indian citizen has a long way to travel in experience and organization to extract from his government reasonable standards of service and consideration.

(vi) *People's Participation*

A recurring theme on the Indian administrative scene has been the question of the people's participation. All shades of opinion, political and administrative, agree that the sharing of power with the people is both desirable and necessary if democracy is to give satisfaction. The experience of an increasing depth of citizenship is the final, and only irreplaceable, bastion for the preservation, growth, and survival of the freedom that democracy seeks to assure.

There is, however, no clear picture as to the extent or the manner of the people's participation in government. One important experiment has been *panchayati raj*. A basic problem that arises out of various attempts at participation is whether this should mean that the people themselves should administer in direct contact with the civil services, and not merely through their ministers. Apart from the difficulty of determining how this should be done, there is a real danger, as in Partap Singh Kairon's regime in the Punjab, that operations across the lines produce a jerky, eccentric administrative effort, which creates suspicion and insecurity rather than stability. Should participation, therefore, mean that while there is the fullest opportunity for debate and discussion, when a particular line of action is decided on the administration should be protected from pressures when implementing it?

Perhaps one of the obstacles to a satisfactory solution is the lack of a strong, viable, and independent system of local government. Today effective local government ends with the state, which is an essential unit of convenient administration, but much too large and distant from the daily impact of ordinary folk to provide opportunity for the expression and education of local opinion in programmes of change and development. There are local bodies, both urban and rural, but these have substantially been creatures of the state government, without an integrity of their own in regard to the responsibility of their leaders, or a proper base of economic independence and viability. The conversion of the district to an independent jurisdiction of local government is possibly the answer. This may well also have the advantage of bringing into a new focus and importance the district officer as an executive primarily responsible to the local leadership. It has been mentioned earlier in this chapter that the district is not only on the decline, but that its administration shows unmistakable signs of disintegration. Nevertheless it remains a vital area for the future, as it is small enough for the source of power, the popular vote, to feel its participation and large enough to be a viable economic development unit for tangible results. Its activities also intimately affect the daily lives of the mass of citizens. *Panchayati raj*, as at present practised, does not provide the substance of independence to the local leadership nor draw on the district officer and his staff as intimately responsible for execution of programmes.

Much greater thought, definition, and careful experiment is obviously required to translate the idea of people's participation into practical programmes that can be understood by the people and executed with both economy and speed. The present position is far from satisfactory; it is also the occasion for constant accusation, from the Prime Minister downwards, that the civil service is insensitive and unresponsive. It does not provide an institutional arena for the district officer to render his accountability nor to view his contribution in terms of its achievements and failures.

THE MORALE OF THE SERVICES

Morale in the services has varied considerably in the post-independence period. It was extremely high immediately following independence, cohesive and strong within the services themselves, powerful in producing efficiency and good work for the country. It is today at a low level. Some factors that have influenced developments may be considered.

The IAS as successor to the ICS is still the premier service. Its numbers have far outgrown those of the ICS. At independence there were 1,500 officers in the ICS, of whom 52 per cent were British. With their departure and partition, India was left with 452. By 1964 the number in the IAS had swelled to 1,974, and on 1 January 1973 the sanctioned strength of the IAS was 3,650 and the number in position 2,597.

In spite of the many difficulties with which the service started and the many changes it coped with, the IAS has stood up to the test, and generally produced an educated officer with high standards of integrity and the capacity for performance. Particularly successful has been the throwing open of the service to women; they have performed well, some individuals exceptionally well; some have succeeded most ably in combining the responsibilities of family life and civil service.

Nonetheless the overall conditions in which the IAS has functioned have changed, and today it is but one of many services in India. The term used about the ICS, 'the service', would no longer be understood in India. Even the IAS would not use it for themselves.

In the services as a whole there have been considerable changes in the means, both sanctions and incentives, available to maintain discipline and to encourage and reward improved efficiency. In the British period, once a man had joined the government his future career depended largely on the judgements of his superiors. That relationship has been broken into in many ways. Legislatures, to whom the government is accountable, tend to insist on impersonal standards for recruitment and promotion. Public Service Commissions consequently play a bigger share in advising on promotions than they did. The assessment of superiors is now only one factor in advancement and no longer the vital one. The atmosphere within departments also makes the exercise of individual judgements by superiors about subordinates difficult, even hazardous. The system of maintaining confidential rolls about each official continues. Annual assessments of performance by the immediate superior of each official go up for review to the head of the office, which includes the minister in regard to senior personnel. Any adverse comments are required to be communicated to the official who may appeal against them. The tradition has developed since independence that there is almost invariably an appeal. In this process the officer who made the adverse remarks frequently finds himself 'on the mat' in explaining and justifying them. The exercise is often complicated, in the case of senior personnel, by a direct 'approach' to the minister by the aggrieved official. The most hair-splitting and subtle arguments are marshalled, and prejudice alleged or implied. The whole business is often messy and time-consuming. Few officers have sustained the practice of frank comment, good or bad, on their subordinates, par- ticularly those with contacts in high places. This again illustrates the point made about vigilance, the lack of common value judgements within the administration. The result is that the administration has lost an important source of judgement for screening its personnel, especially at the most senior levels where leadership is involved and an assessment must be based at least partly on intangibles, and to that extent may even be subjective, though not necessarily for that reason incorrect.

In the case of rank and file employees, service associations and unions have gained strength. These are frequently chaired by politicians, labour leaders, and social workers. Decisions are arrived at by com- promise, affected by politics, and applied by rule of thumb. It is difficult for civil service heads to exercise any degree of initiative and freedom in the control and discipline of their subordinates. In 1973 in the UP the Provincial Armed Constabulary went as far as armed revolt, which had to be quelled with the help of the army. The Chief Minister had to step down from office. This is an extreme case but is sympto- matic of the daily difficulties the administration faces, at ordinary levels, in maintaining efficiency and morale.

The relationship between superior and subordinate has been eroded and with it the bonds of control, supervision, and disciplinary sanction of the services by the services. With it has also been dissipated the bond of attachment, interest, and loyalty, between officers and men. Except in the army, and to an extent in the police, that relationship is no longer an active institutional force in the services.

Many officials complain frankly that they are unable to extract the degree and quality of discipline and efficiency that they need. They express themselves helpless in rendering good service to their clientele. They complain that as a result a few men carry an unfair burden of the work load, and their organizations do not achieve the strength, the cohesion, and the public service that the payroll would justify.

Underlying these developments is the public inclination, shared even by the political masters, to regard the administrative services as entities on their own, not as instruments created by the people and governments of India. The isolation of the civil service is thus accentuated; it becomes in situations of crisis readily available as a scapegoat; *esprit de corps* and the will to persevere are discouraged and problematic.

'SWAN SONG' FOR THE ICS

By an amendment of the Indian Constitution in 1972 the clause guaranteeing a continuation of the conditions of the 'Secretary of State's Services' was withdrawn. This was generally described and viewed as putting an end to the 'privileges of the ICS'. In fact there were differences, not privileges, governing some details of the service conditions of the ICS as compared with the other all-India services. The only real extra was that the ICS officer retired after thirty-five years work, which meant usually at an age that varied between fifty-seven and sixty-one years, depending on where and at what age he entered the ICS, while other services retired at the age of fifty-eight. Most ICS officers in fact retired between fifty-eight and fifty-nine; a few have even received a longer tenure by the amendment. Considering the circumstances, the amendment was futile. There were less than fifty officers left in the ICS when it was passed, and the youngest of these would have retired in the normal course in 1979. The problem was therefore infinitesimal and the change, coming as it did twenty-five years after independence, had the absurdity of killing a fly with a machine gun. The amendment was, however, a clear pointer to the Government of India's markedly changed attitude towards the ICS, part of its ideological approach to the administrative services in general.

The ICS is the only service in India, perhaps in the world, whose remuneration and benefits have remained static in the whole period since 1947, a time of continuous inflation. All other services in India, including the IAS, have received, in one way or another, improved emoluments or benefits. The ICS, with few exceptions, however, chose to remain with the government. Those few who left have invariably earned better outside it, usually in industry.

The governments immediately following independence, and since, have relied heavily on the few ICS men who remain. The service has carried its full burden of responsibility (and the use of its experience and skill) in helping to establish India as an independent nation, and in the building of the institutional base for democracy. It has also been associated with commercial and financial organizations in government and the public sector. India has the distinction of having contributed more than its share of competent persons to international organizations, and many of these have been from the ICS. In return the ICS was on the whole well treated and well esteemed by its political masters and the public. Men from its ranks have been repeatedly selected for difficult and delicate political-administrative assignments and this continues to be the experience of the handful that remains.

Given the association of the ICS with colonial rule it is understandable that the recognition accorded to it and the reliance placed on it after independence has been somewhat clandestine and underplayed and at times been accompanied by hints of hostility and resentment. The last found formal expression in the constitutional amendment of 1972.

Philip Woodruff, the biographer of the ICS, subtitled his two volumes *The Founders* and *The Guardians*. Perhaps 'The Scavengers'* would be an appropriate title for a post-independence volume about them. The ICS rendered yeoman service in this period in removing the debris, the potential untidiness, the possible disorder, facing the new democracy; they helped to keep the environment free, even clean. India has always had two great cleansers, one the scorching sun that dries and dissipates much that is filthy, the other the vulture, a scavenger. This ungainly, unbeautiful, and little-loved bird has, nevertheless, rendered 'great and meritorious service'.

CONCLUSION

Is it possible to see any overall meaning in the specific developments in the administration outlined here? I have no comprehensive thesis to propose; what I offer is a personal point of view and no more than an indication.

The first fact that stands out is that the administration in India has in many directions rendered excellent service. Some aspects of its success have been described in this book. The relief and rehabilitation of the displaced in the Punjab (Chapter 4), the construction of the Bhakra Dam and the Chandigarh capital (Chapter 5), and developments in the administration of food (Chapter 3) are some examples of new and difficult tasks performed with good results. In other spheres the administration has not done such good work and has on occasion even had manifest failure, as in the re-introduction of the monopoly in foodgrains (Appendix I).

The administrative system may therefore be assessed as capable of satisfying performance. It is a good machine, an organization that with time and stability could become more sensitive to the needs of its ordinary consumers and achieve great performance. This in spite of the fact that the years since independence have been a period of vast expansion and of adaptation of the structure to cater for the needs of parliamentary democracy and a federal Union.

When has the administration done well, and when badly? It is possible to find cause and effect in the quality of the political direction it has received. Where this has been cohesive in objective and clear

* Dr Hugh Tinker, who kindly read and made suggestions on the manuscript of this book, commented ' "The Scavengers". Isn't this a bit cruel? How about "The Goalkeepers"?'

about values the administration has responded with adequate, sometimes excellent, efficiency; where these have not been forthcoming, it has tarnished its image, been blamed, and perhaps also been responsible for the dissatisfaction. This point is vividly illustrated in the career of Partap Singh Kairon as chief minister of the Punjab (Chapter 7), when the administration achieved great success in the development of the state, but in the same period and with the same leader earned a degree of suspicion and attracted a volume of opposition that brought Kairon's power tumbling down over his own head.

It seems correct to draw the conclusion that this is not so far an administrative system that can in respect of most of its work be expected to carry on on its own, irrespective of the character and quality of the political leadership. It may well be that India has not had the experience to develop such a self-sustaining administrative system. It may be that the diversities of the country, even between various classes in the same area, make difficult commonly accepted arenas of government immune from the adverse influence of poor political leadership. Whatever the reasons, and these are obviously complex, Indian administration seems vitally dependent, in spirit and practice, on its master's voice, on the political mandate.

One reservation to this must be recorded in that various states have been, for brief periods of usually less than a year at a time, under President's rule, when the constitution has been suspended and the administration carried on by the civil services under the supervision of the Governor, frequently assisted by senior civil service advisers. It has been the invariable experience that during these periods administrative standards and efficiency have improved. This, however, does not detract from the conclusion stated, for these are usually short periods, following upon a crisis or major deterioration, and during them no major policy decisions are taken. They are vacuums in the normal political and administrative life of the community.

The specific requirements which in this setting make for good administration can be stated quite simply, though to obtain them through the political system is more difficult, and involves the whole value system, disciplines, and aims of society. The strictly administrative requirements or pre-conditions are:

(i) At any given time, a clear definition of policy by the government in power;

(ii) In the defining of policy, a careful examination of the contradictions that may be involved both within a given policy as well as between it and other policies. In this matter a great deal of work requires to be done in harmonizing short or shorter-term possibilities with long-term objectives. Policy must face hard choices and make them clearly, setting out what it will immediately sacrifice, how it will 'make do', in order to meet practical needs;

(iii) The official, having been informed of policy, must be assured a degree of freedom to implement it, so that he is both squarely and fully responsible for doing so and accountable for success, shortfall, or failure;

(iv) The hard core of normal administrative activities must be permitted to proceed whatever the party in power, and whoever the boss. The community must build up fields of activity where the rule of law is not in fact in jeopardy from politics.

These are all aspects of achieving cohesion and direction for the administrative process, of finding the point where politics and administration may best meet in order to consolidate and protect the continuity of administrative practice that ensures services for the citizen. This is in some ways as simple as a problem of balance and discipline, of keeping the administrative structure in good running order. Without this it seems difficult for politics to produce the thoughtful debate and, flowing from it, the programmes of change and development that India will need for many years to come.

The administrative system today may perhaps be assessed as 'the plastic frame', potentially pliable in the pursuit of policy. Even such a frame needs joints and hubs, points at which flows are stopped, retarded, or increased. Only a basic structure that is well maintained and that can be taken for granted can sustain on behalf of the citizen the regulatory systems, the amenities, and the services that have already been achieved. It is only such an organization that might then also be accepted with confidence as the instrument of change and improvement.

APPENDIX I

THE FAILURE OF THE WHEAT MONOPOLY, 1973–1974*

I have thought it useful to add a brief description of the attempt at monopoly procurement in 1973–74 even though this did not come within my personal administrative experience. It illustrates how sound the food policy formulated after 1943 had been; how dangerous it was to depart from its principles; and throws light on administrative relations in India in the 1970s.

The story of Chapter 3 ends at the decontrol of 1954. This continued well into 1972. During this period significant developments took place in food policy and administration. In 1965 the Food Corporation of India was established as a central government corporation to handle both the import of foodgrains and the purchase of 'buffer stocks' in the internal markets, at times through the state governments. In this way the centre came to control normally at least two to four and at times even ten million tonnes of foodgrains in its direct custody.

A price support policy to encourage farmers to increase food production was introduced. The support price of wheat by 1970 was Rs 76.00 per quintal, at which price government undertook to buy all stocks offered. The ruling market price was generally somewhat higher than this. As against this price Punjab had been purchasing wheat in 1950 at Rs 36.00 per quintal. The price support policy undoubtedly encouraged production.

Indeed there was a dramatic increase in production from the mid-1960s. The causes of this were varied and are not discussed here. The most significant factor in the case of wheat was the use of high yielding seed generally called 'Mexican'. The highest production of wheat in India before the 'green revolution' had been 12.3 million tonnes in 1964; normally the crop was smaller, ten to eleven millions. These figures were now improved to 16.5 million tonnes in 1968, 18.7 in the next year, and over 23 million tonnes in 1970. The promise was such that the Government of India announced that India could stop imports in the early 1970s. So confident was the food outlook that Bombay in 1971 withdrew its rationing of wheat which had been started in 1943 and maintained after decontrol.

The political context also changed with the Indira Gandhi regime from 1967 and dramatically from 1969. The election of the President

* See Chapter 3.

that year split the ruling Congress party. In the process the Prime Minister presented to the country a posture of advanced radicalism and nationalization. Following the split she maintained the power of her minority government with the crucial help of the Communist vote and party machine. In 1971 she was able to win a massive vote in her favour in the mid-term poll, achieving a two-thirds majority in the Lok Sabha. She now had, however, what amounted to an undefined alliance with the Communist party and its methods. External pressures cemented these trends. The agony of Bangladesh continuing through the whole of 1971 seemed to vindicate the treaty of friendship with the USSR signed in August of that year. These events culminated in the brilliant diplomatic and military operation that defeated Pakistan at the end of 1971. Mrs Gandhi was at the very peak of power and popularity. The elections in most of the states in 1972 brought further strength to Mrs Gandhi's Congress.

The economy, however, had been put to considerable strain. The partial failure of the monsoon in 1972 made it evident in the autumn that there would again be food difficulties. The government appeared well poised to meet these, backed as it was with mass support in both the Union and the state governments, and with a buffer stock of nine million tonnes of foodgrains on 1 July 1972. This position of strength remained unexploited and was in the event dissipated in the massive and manifest failure of the attempted monopoly procurement in 1973–74.

At the annual meeting of the Congress Party at Bidhan Nagar, in Calcutta, in December 1972, it was resolved that government should introduce monopoly procurement of wheat from the crop year starting April 1973, and of rice in October; also that the wholesale trade in these foodgrains should be eliminated and replaced by a government agency. These decisions had some remarkable features. It was evident that they had not been considered in any depth by the party itself but only proposed and pushed by a few of the communist-inspired top leaders and Mrs Gandhi. When some chief ministers of the Congress party pointed out difficulties of a practical kind, they were dealt with almost on the basis of a party whip which treated dissent or doubt as reactionary resistance to progress. Administratively, the decision was highly ambitious involving as it did, at short notice, not only the responsibility for handling huge quantities of wheat but also doing so without the complex machinery of the wholesale trade which was to be replaced. These two operations could have been staggered.

But the most remarkable fact was the omission of any mention of rationing. This indeed was a question of practical principle, as previous experience had shown rationing to be an inescapable condition of successful procurement. It is obvious that adequate administrative consultation did not precede the announcement of policy. There were a number of experienced food administrators in the country, even in Delhi, who knew that a procurement drive of any size, inevitably a monopoly, entailed rationing. These were two sides of the same medal, and that had also been the main burden of the two Policy Committees on the subject, the Gregory report of 1943, re-emphasized and underlined by the Thirumala Rao report of 1950.

Why is rationing an essential corollary to monopoly procurement in Indian circumstances? This may be explained briefly as follows:

(i) India is a marginal importer of foodgrains, in quantity averaging in the twenty years 1951 to 1971 less than four million tonnes a year, against an internal production now amounting to over 100 million tonnes, and even up to 108 millions in 1970–71. While the imported grain is vital, both as tilting the balance to adequacy and on the other hand as requiring foreign exchange so crucially needed by the economy, the success of the distribution system depends on the internal surpluses available. The imported quantity is only a palliative to bolster up and meet the marginal extra.

(ii) The internal surplus is produced, and initially held, by literally millions of farmers, mostly in small quantities. These farmers have to be induced to part with it at the normal time at a reasonable price. Their numbers are so large that it is impracticable to work a monopoly by merely passing an unenforceable law requiring them to deliver surpluses; indeed to prove that a particular surplus had not come in would in itself be difficult. Therefore conditions have to be created to convince the farmer that he should part with his surplus.

(iii) The essential condition to induce the marketing of a surplus is adequate stability in the price and supply position. That in turn can only be created, in circumstances of shortage and monopoly, if the government effectively removes the intensity of demand by providing a guarantee of a stable ration to the consumer, particularly in the concentrated urban deficit areas. Rationing alone can produce the slack in the fierce demand for food that will convince the farmer that he should market his surplus at a reasonable price.

(iv) The alternative should be coercion, but the scale of coercion required would be impractical. Another alternative would be the 'levy', the calculation of each producer's surplus and its collection. This was worked in Bombay after 1943, but generally requires an organization so large, dealing with each village and each producer, that it is administratively difficult, even apart from the problem of honest assessments and administration on so vast a scale. Therefore the monopoly utilized in India generally has been at the market, not the village, and for this a rationing system, at least in all towns, has been essential.

(v) Even apart from these considerations, it is logically necessary—and this becomes physically manifest immediately in food—that if government as the sole controller of grain creates a monopoly at any stage of marketing, it must create a distribution agency for all persons to be fed beyond that stage. Where grain is short, the most orderly and economic distribution would be rationing.

From April 1973 arrangements were made for the wheat monopoly. Each state was cordoned off as a zone and the law prescribed that wheat might be purchased in markets only by the government and its agents. Retailers authorized by the state could store and sell limited quantities under government direction. It was apparently assumed that the fair price shops would meet the distribution problem, even though these shops neither guaranteed a regular supply nor prevented the citizen from making purchases on his own. The responsibility to supply, and the obligation by the consumer to accept no other supply, were both lacking. In the absence of rationing, which provides precisely these twin points of security to system and consumer, there was a vacuum.

This vacuum was filled by fact and apprehension. At times supplies were not available; even when and where they were apprehension for their continuity created a run on them. These were difficulties, which grew steadily, from the start of the monopoly. The government met the situation by allowing retailers to purchase limited amounts from the market to feed their customers, and by allowing customers to buy direct from the farmer for personal consumption. The farmer was now convinced that he had not one buyer in the government for his wheat, but several. In places the consumer, when he could not lay his hands on supplies, panicked further. The running sore of distress, now here, now there, became the dominant distribution theme.

As the season advanced there were food riots, first in Nagpur, then in Bombay, later in Mysore. In Kerala education was shut down after students attacked grain trucks. Supplies were rushed to distress areas; the movement of 'special trainloads' was publicized in the press, and over the government-operated radio. There was drama about the movement of food. The wheat 'monopoly' had become a shambles within weeks of its start.

On 31 August Fakhruddin Ali Ahmad, the Food minister, reporting to the party said that the government had purchased to that date 600–700,000 tonnes less than it did in a free market in the previous year. The buffer stock of nine million tonnes had been reduced, after accounting for new purchases, to four million tonnes. He did not say, but the figures implied, that the situation was not under control, and that there was no certainty as to what was going out and what could come in. Meanwhile the import market had become more difficult and expensive. The government was eventually driven to such straits as to 'borrow' two million tonnes of wheat from the USSR, on terms which remain undefined. Elements of farce were added to the situation in the attempt to find scapegoats or palliatives. UP even announced travelling facilities for state legislators to induce the arrival of wheat at the markets.

In mid-September 1973 the government announced that the planned rice monopoly (to start in October 1973) was postponed. The Prime Minister put the blame squarely on the administration. She said:

... the administrative machinery was not good enough to shoulder the responsibilities of distribution of rice if the wholesale trade in rice was nationalized immediately. A greater involvement of the Congress organization and the people was required. The present deferment was only a temporary adjustment to a special situation. (*Statesman Weekly*, 22 September 1973)

In wheat difficulties continued. Prices of wheat and foodgrains generally had gone up phenomenally during the period, influencing as they do in India, the whole price structure. In March 1974 the Gujarat state government, in the hands of the Congress party, was suspended, the legislature dissolved on public insistence, and President's rule enforced. At the end of that month signs of a similar predicament in Bihar were evident. These events followed agitation and riots, during which over a hundred people were killed. In both states food prices and availability had been the important trigger to these explosions.

On 4 April 1974 the year's account in wheat monopoly was struck. The government decided that it would not be continued for the new crop year 1974–75. The support price of wheat was raised to Rs 105.00 per quintal; forward projections estimated a market price during the year touching Rs 150.00. The attempted monopoly thus coincided with the largest inflation in price since controls started in 1943.

The tragedy is that these developments were avoidable. Administratively the country had both the knowledge and the personnel to introduce and establish a successful monopoly for wheat in the circumstances of 1973. It had substantially started and administered one throughout the country in more difficult circumstances following 1943. This had continued down to 1947 and even 1950 and then been gradually eroded and abandoned by 1954.

The task was made more difficult in 1973 by the decision simultaneously to eliminate the wholesale trade. But what made it impossible to achieve was the evasion and avoidance of rationing, without which monopoly cannot work. The sequence of events and the ultimate breakdown of policy suggest a lack of rapport, even of adequate communication, between political masters and administrative experts. The latter certainly knew what was required; they could have achieved it during an agricultural year which started with nine million tonnes of food in the centre's stores. Policy collapsed because it failed to provide for rationing. It was as simple as that.

The explanation must belong squarely to the political sphere. Decisions were obviously made at an ideological level, oblivious and impatient of practical and administrative considerations. The policy was cloaked in the mantle of destroying vested interests; why not the wholesale trade? It was rumoured at the time that one of the ministers described them as the symbol of the petty bourgeoisie which must be destroyed, sooner rather than later. The consumer did not like rationing, so why not have a monopoly without it? It seems, however absurd this may sound, that euphoria, sentiment, and prejudice determined the content of policy with little consideration for established logic and fact.

The confidence of the country in the government was shaken to the core by these events. Conditions bordering on anarchy emerged in some areas. An opportunity to get a grip on the food situation was lost, indeed even abandoned. The consequences may be calamitous. In the process the administrative machinery unjustly lost reputation and confidence. It was, at the highest level, held responsible for failure successfully to administer a policy which, defined and conceived as it was, was bound to fail, as it did from the very start.

APPENDIX II

THE KASHMIR ISSUE*

It is not part of this book to attempt any systematic analysis of the
Kashmir problem. I was, however, working in Jammu and Kashmir
during the major confrontation between India and Pakistan in 1965,
and in the position of an intimate, inside observer, indeed even a
participant, in some of the events and decisions of the time. It seems
appropriate, therefore, to add some comment on the situation.

In the course of the war of 1965 it was clear that almost every one of
the assumptions on which Pakistan apparently acted, in taking the
initiative at that time in Kashmir, proved false. Pakistan had assumed
that the people of the valley, where it concentrated its main effort,
would make common cause with it, and would assist in plunging the
state government into disorder. Yet it failed to receive a significant
response, even though it had been careful not to repeat the mistakes of
1947. This time it launched massive infiltration rather than direct
attack, and the infiltrators behaved like disciplined soldiers and did not
indulge in looting and arson. They were well supplied with money and
were willing, indeed anxious, to pay for the goods and services they
demanded. But they found it difficult even to obtain the Kashmiri-
speaking guides they needed to assist their movements in desolate
mountain terrain. Sadiq's government did not have to take any special
or extreme measures to meet any dissidence on the part of residents of
the valley. Indeed in villages people, while briefly subdued in the
physical presence of the infiltrators, kept the administration and the
army informed of all movement and activity.

A second Pakistani assumption seemed to be that there was scope for
taking advantage of potential tension within the Indian army. Considerable propaganda was directed by Pakistan at the Sikhs on the basis
that they were restive and dissatisfied comrades in arms alongside the
Hindu majority. Perhaps this hope had been encouraged by the rather
extreme positions and speeches of Sikh politicians regarding *Punjabi
Suba*, which Kairon had so strongly opposed. But whatever Sikh
opinion might have been on internal politics there were no differences
at all in attitudes to Pakistan. The Indian army was quite uninfluenced
by the attempt to create any cleavage of sentiment within it.

Pakistan had also perhaps assumed that India would attempt to

* See Chapter 8.

contain the war within Jammu and Kashmir and would not launch a counter-offensive against Pakistan itself. That it did open offensives on the Sialkot and Lahore fronts was possibly the only tangible achievement of the war for India. It proved to both Pakistan, and to the Indian public, that the unity of India, including Jammu and Kashmir, was one and indivisible.

Nor did the threats and sabre-rattling of China materialize in specific assistance to Pakistan, though they undoubtedly caused grave anxiety to India. China, however, proved unwilling to help its proclaimed ally to the point of force.

Does the defeat of these many assumptions mean anything in terms of the heart of the Kashmir problem? The political will, in the context of nationality in the Kashmir valley, had now been put to the severest test twice since independence. In 1947 Pakistan-supported tribesmen had arrived at the precincts of Srinagar, having defeated and scattered the Maharaja's army, and sacked Baramulla. There was at the time not a single Indian soldier, or even policeman, in Jammu and Kashmir. It was the leaders of the people in the valley who decided that India should be asked to defend Srinagar. Indian troops arrived at Srinagar by Dakota, in a situation where not a single plane could have landed but for local civilian goodwill, and indeed insistence, that it should. The valley had firmly and dramatically declared for the Indian connection. By 1965 there had been a long time to reassess the position. Much wisdom, and even more verbiage, had been expended on the Kashmir issue. Yet the planned and organized initiative of Pakistan to disrupt and then seize the valley with the help of the local population proved futile. The response of the people produced no shift in Pakistan's favour. The valley had again confirmed its choice of 1947.

The fact remains that, in the relevant councils of the world and even in the inner thoughts of Indians, there is doubt whether the Kashmir valley is, by choice of its people, a unit of federal India. Much of this is due to the adamant insistence of Pakistan that this Muslim majority area, contiguous to it, is necessarily bound by sentiment and interest with Muslim Pakistan.

There are, however, other factors that merit consideration. Pakistan, in support of its claim, has over the years created a vested and largely economic interest in the state. There are paid agents all over Kashmir regularly financed by Pakistan. They may almost be said to constitute a paid service, organized at varying levels, from high-ranking *mullas* (priests) in receipt of regular fees to lower cadres of minions used for special, often violent, purposes. Nor are these agents exclusively Muslim. In some of the Hindu majority areas it is obviously an advantage to seek assistance from the comparative anonymity of the major local religion. In such a poor state incentives of this kind are by no means unattractive. The events of 1965 seemed to confirm this view from another angle. While the infiltrators were in the valley they received hardly any support. Once they were driven out agitational activity was revived on behalf of Pakistan. It was as if the Pakistan 'civil service' had returned from leave taken for the duration of the armed conflict.

Perhaps there is a degree of justification for both Pakistan's insistence, and Indian doubts, in the fact that the valley is indeed a special cultural and historic entity, and does not correspond to the norms that Pakistan and India have been accustomed to consider as governing the reactions and relations between the two religions. I have attempted in Chapter 8 to describe how cultural patterns and relations in the valley are in many ways unique and distinct from those of the rest of the sub-continent. It should not be surprising, therefore, that these have led to a choice of nationality, twice confirmed in crisis, on a basis which Pakistan cannot understand and will not accept, and about which even marginal Indian opinion has expressed doubt.

Observations as categorical as this cannot, however, be made of the Poonch-Rajouri area, where communal patterns correspond more nearly to those of sub-continent history. In 1965 it was only in this part of the state that the infiltrators penetrated comparatively effectively and drove a wedge between the two religious communities. Had similar conditions and reactions been available to them in the valley, 1965 would have been a very different story.

APPENDIX III

'OUR PRESENT DISCONTENTS'[*]

The vital dependence of the Indian administrative system on political direction, even in the provision of routine regulatory and amenity services, has been vividly illustrated in the period 1967 to 1974. There were already signs that paralysis was overcoming the government in important policy decisions at the time when I resigned from the ICS at the end of 1971; I have mentioned some of these in Chapter 9. Since then India has proceeded further to what is now generally agreed, even within the Indian government, to be the gravest crisis since independence. Administration has virtually broken down in some states and is at best limping along in most of the country. Many of these manifestations have emerged more fully since I left the civil service and do not strictly belong to this book. They do, however, throw light on the administrative developments I have described, and I venture, therefore, to include this Appendix.

Three sets of processes may be traced during this period, working up to deep crisis, more evident and worsening since the elections to parliament in 1971 and to some of the state assemblies in 1972:

(i) Actions taken by the Union government and the Congress Party in power in several of the states, have dealt a severe blow to the constitutional, political, and administrative order built up by India since independence. Public order and accepted public values have been shaken;

(ii) There are so far no indications that the shake-up of established norms and fundamentals has been accompanied by any consistent body of alternative practical policy or direction. The changes that have been made do not appear to be directed to any clearly determined public purpose;

(iii) There is thus a vacuum of policy, purpose, and direction, producing a now rapid deterioration in administration.

I have already described the many developments in Indian administration which have loosened its structure to more decentralized and diversified institutional and executive agencies. I have suggested that this was not only inevitable but desirable in our transformation from a colonial order to a democratic, federal Union. The danger, however,

[*] See Chapter 10.

remains that unless there is well-conceived direction to consolidate and lead the administration, the processes of disrepair and disintegration can multiply fast, and become a problem in themselves. That is what seems to have been happening. There has been a literal breakdown of the administrative machine, at the most ordinary levels of performance, in UP in 1973, in Gujarat in March 1974, and in Bihar shortly thereafter. I mention these states because events there have reached a point of recognized formal action and no one can question the facts. The same tendencies, however, are evident elsewhere and there is constant and general apprehension that they may not merely remain the running sore of maladministration but actually erupt in crisis. There is also evidence that while the immediate causes and events may centre round local matters, it is from the background of the all-India context that problems originate.

Let me consider briefly some of the jolts that the system has received, starting with the election of a new President in August 1969, following the death of Zakir Husain in May. The official candidate of the Congress Party, Sanjiva Reddy, whose nomination papers were signed by the Prime Minister, was repudiated by her at the last moment in her fight for absolute control of her party. She then supported V. V. Giri, the independent candidate, and her own party's nominee was defeated in the campaign of intrigue and manipulation that accompanied this decision. The Indian public, agog with excitement and thrilled by the scent of 'the kill', was witness to the fact that a new non-ethic now determined the politics of power at the highest levels of leadership. 'My darling daughter', said Mrs Giri to the Prime Minister!

Following the split in the party resulting from this, the new Congress was without an absolute majority in parliament, for the first time since independence. The Prime Minister's crucial ally became the Communist Party of India (CPI), and the beginnings of a link with it were forged, influencing the nature and style of both politics and administrative decision. Popular feeling was worked up, even inflamed, in a sustained attack on 'vested interests', which seemed to include all parties and persons in opposition to the Prime Minister, most persons among the educated minority, the managerial, bureaucratic, and industrial leadership, the critical sections of the press—with the princes thrown in as feudal fodder.

In the near hysterical conditions thus created, the country breathed a sigh of relief when, after the elections to parliament in 1971, Mrs Gandhi emerged with a convincing and solid two-thirds majority. This seemed to portend a return to settled, defined policy and development. This appeared confirmed by events in Bangladesh during 1971, culminating in India's first manifest victory in war in modern times. The state assembly elections of 1972 reflected public admiration for Mrs

Gandhi, returning the new Congress in greater numbers. She now had an overwhelming mandate for decisive policy. These results also reversed the position of the general election of 1967, when Congress lost a large number of seats and the mid-term poll in five states in February 1969, which confirmed the downhill trend of the party.

But public opinion and confidence, even in the rank and file of the new Congress itself as rousingly expressed in the annual session at Bidhan Nagar (Calcutta) in December 1972, were badly shaken by the means employed to collect election moneys and sometimes by the conduct of the elections themselves. Ajit Bhattacharjea, now an editor of the *Times of India*, referred to this in an article of 15 July 1973, in the *Illustrated Weekly*:

Money has been collected for election and other party purposes before, but never on the scale and in the manner it was for the *Lok Sabha* election in 1971, and the State Assembly elections a year later. *Crores* [one crore is ten million rupees] are known to have been extracted from the business community, but there is no account of these transactions. The entire sum was paid in black money; no legal accounts were kept . . . so a premium was placed on massive dishonesty and corruption and the parallel black money economy—with all its degrading social and economic effects—was legitimized.

There are few who would contradict this view. Congress itself passed in 1969 the law banning donations from companies to political parties. Since the election of 1971 it has been, without much secrecy, the main recipient of such donations. As it is obviously safer to pay illegal donations to the party in power, the law has been enforced by it with an absent-mindedness that ensures that it is practically the sole beneficiary of its violation. The scope for abuse, even private gain, is obvious.

This series of events has irretrievably destroyed the moral bond and faith that undoubtedly existed between the electorate and the leadership of Congress, forged by Gandhi and consolidated by Nehru. There have been individual Congressmen who lacked integrity in almost all the states, especially after Congress came to power, but never before had the public had reason to believe, even to suspect, that its top leadership could be involved or tarnished.

The government now proceeded to a series of repudiations of guarantees defined in the constitution. I have mentioned the abolition of 'the privileges of the ICS' (Chapter 10). A constitutional amendment of 1971 extinguished the covenant with the princes, the overwhelming majority of whom came voluntarily into the Union in 1947–48, and were guaranteed defined prerogatives, including a privy purse, by the constitution. The amendment abrogated what amounted to a solemn treaty that had achieved the unity of India without bloodshed. Nor did it appear necessary, as the princes had indicated that they would be willing to work out with the government a suitable compromise to meet what was described as 'the changed conditions'. Fundamental rights were also the subject of constitutional amendments (1971), the main effect of which was to change the term 'compensation', for the take-over of property by the state, to the word 'amount', thus handing to government the power to place an arbitrary value on the property of citizens.

While these amendments added only infinitesimal amounts to the public coffers, they did create an ideological stir, which however lost its impact when no follow-up emerged in the shape of effective programmes to benefit the common man, or in a realistic recognition of an economic situation which had been deteriorating steadily. Even optimistic assessments hold that the economy is at best at a stand-still. We have noticed how the food monopoly has almost doubled the price of wheat in only fifteen months (Appendix I).

Erosion of the federal principle, round which the Indian constitution is built, has also taken place. An article of 16 July 1973 in the *Times of India* says:

Since Mrs Gandhi became Prime Minister seven and a half years ago, the Centre has invoked President's rule twenty-two times to take over the administration of States. In the previous 16 years after the Constitution took effect, these emergency powers were used 10 times.

State governments have become somewhat like municipalities, playthings of the party in power at the Union. Confidence has been shaken, responsibility and accountability are impaired; state politicians are no longer compelled to mend the fences that have broken within their jurisdiction, but instead can, in the commonly used phrase, 'look to the centre' for escape.

I have thus far mentioned subjects which refer to politics and the constitution. Meddling with fundamentals creates a series of chain reactions, and there have been repercussions on the public services. In the 1969 crisis and its aftermath the services were labelled conservative and reactionary. There was a call for a 'committed civil service', although the term was not defined. The bureaucracy has been placed under a cloud with the encouragement or at least the acquiescence of the government itself. I have referred in Appendix I to the Prime Minister's declaration that the administration was not of adequate calibre to make monopoly procurement a success.

In 1973 the rising tempo of government-directed criticism of the courts was highlighted by widespread protests when a new chief justice, No. 4 on the Supreme Court, was appointed in preference to his seniors. The government's spokesmen on the issue—these included one of its ablest ministers, Kumaramangalam (now deceased), who even produced a monograph on the subject—maintained that it had the right to appoint judges who had the correct committed values. Senior lawyers, on the other hand, assessed this as a move to 'pack' the judiciary at the highest level, to start the practice of 'people's justice', associated with authoritarian regimes. These fears gained support from the fact that government representatives had kept up a criticism of the untamed press and in 1971 the Ministry of Information and Broadcasting had gone so far as to circulate proposals for what was termed 'diffusion' of the ownership and management of the press that would have amounted to thinly veiled control; this in India which had prided itself on the health, variety, and freedom of its press since independence.

Meanwhile it was also becoming clearer that the Prime Minister's regime relied heavily on intelligence organization. A police officer in that branch has been raised to the full status of a secretary to the Government of India. His name is Kao (pronounced 'cow') and in the corridors of the Secretariat—where there were also now strains and whispers of fear—his henchmen are referred to as 'cowboys'.

Nor has the link of the ruling Congress with the CPI been understood by, or explained to, the public. Certain terms and phrases of a familiar type have become current coinage; 'right reaction and left adventurism', 'uncommitted intellectuals', 'foreign agents', 'the nefarious activities of the CIA'—an opposition MP, Piloo Mody, by way of parody, entered the House with the label 'CIA' on his coat!— this is the jargon used by government to explain away its failures. The Prime Minister, when pressed, has taken pains to explain that she is not a Communist. But members of her own party have found it difficult to understand the working alliance with the Communists. One development in the situation followed from the support given by Congress to Communist candidates in the elections of early 1974 in the UP and Orissa. The *Overseas Hindustan Times* of 21 February 1974 reported:

. . . Congress President Shankar Dayal Sharma said that it was the duty of Congressmen to support the Communist party candidates . . . In Cuttack, in Orissa, Prime Minister Indira Gandhi advised voters to support the CPI wherever they were seeking election, because the domestic and foreign policies of the two parties were identical.

There has been in this and related ways a thorough shock to established values and settled conventions in Indian political and administrative life. Large sections of the public were apparently prepared for these, indeed even enthusiastically supported the changes, in the belief that they were the beginning of a bigger, more definite, and faster programme of development and good administration. In the period before the election of 1971 there was considerable support for the Prime Minister in what was seen as a fight against conservative interests within her own party. It was partly because of this that the people voted massively for her. They believed that the victory furnished the fullest mandate for a new deal and for clear leadership. The tragedy is that nothing has emerged and there has been a steadily accelerating decline both in the economic situation and clarity of objective, policy, and purpose. There has been a great deal of talk and many promises regarding the 'social content' of future planning; some *ad hoc* schemes with little practical content, like a 'crash programme for employment', have appeared on the stage, but the party and government have failed to produce a plan, or even individual programmes, that carry conviction. Indeed each outline or approach to a new plan, or draft of one, has proved unreal and abortive even before the ink had dried on the paper. It is difficult to avoid the conclusion that the many moves in the political and constitutional sphere which have shaken confidence were in fact designed and perpetrated merely to rally feeling and support for the maintenance, consolidation, and increase of power. The leadership does not lead. It gives the appearance of depending on *ad hoc* urges, strutting and striding across the administrative stage now littered with the damaged and destroyed props of the past, mindlessly determined to retain the limelight.

In this situation, in which hard-won ground is pathetically lost and not made good by gains of new advances, all the bogeys of Indian history take shape, acquire flesh and vigour.

There is an increase in authoritarianism. In the absence of policy, persons seek the mandate from the mere words or indications of the powerful, particularly the PM. India again 'hangs on the lips of the monarch'. In some circles the Prime Minister is referred to familiarly as '*malika*' (the empress).

There is an increase in centralization, both political and administrative. Comparative trivia get referred upwards, for the overall context to determine action is not known, and it might be hazardous to assume a position. I recall that my own leave application, for a fairly routine matter of four months between two jobs, had to be brought to the notice of the Prime Minister by the cabinet secretary. Even the allotment of government housing to an official may become the subject of orders at the highest level. In keeping with this even senior administrators often say quite frankly that they cannot state what the policy is regarding applications submitted to them. 'There have been so many individual cases' is the explanation. Decisions in the secretariat are shaped by the cult of 'consensus', an attempt to shuffle towards a distribution of responsibility over a number of officials rather than a chiselled recommendation from each officer concerned, defining in 'noting' his cumulative experience in advice to his superiors.

There has inevitably been an encouragement, even the creation, of expectations. This has been unaccompanied by a call for work and greater production, nor even an explanation that this may be required by India—now, and for many years. It has been a time of strained labour-management relations, and the loss of much working time, even in the public sector.

The forces of disintegration in the administration have gathered strength. Ordinary services, like post, water, electricity, and transport are uneven and their periodic, even frequent, breakdowns now tend to be accepted as an incidence of Indian administration. The same is true of lawlessness.

Yet as recently as 1971, in the war with Pakistan, the administration responded, like a single orchestra, to play the complicated and precisely synchronized tune that war demands. It is indeed leadership and direction that is lacking, not capacity. Will direction be made available before administration disintegrates so far that it must be rebuilt? This indeed is a crisis of large dimensions, in which the chief sorrow is that now, unlike in the past, it is imposed by Indians on Indians. We have to find the answer.

INDEX